THE STORY OF CHRISTIANITY

Tim Dowley

A LION BOOK

Copyright © 1981 Lion Publishing
Published by
Lion Publishing
Icknield Way, Tring, Herts, England
ISBN 0 85648 245 5
Albatross Books
PO Box 320, Sutherland, NSW 2232,
Australia
ISBN 0 86760 255 4

First edition 1981

The photographs in this book are
reproduced by permission of the following
photographers and organizations:
Barnaby's Picture Library, facing page 1,
pages 12, 13, 25 (above), 42-43, 47, 48, 49;
Billy Graham Evangelistic Association, page
55; Bibliothèque Nationale, Paris/Bisonte,
pages 26-27, 50; BBC Hulton Picture Library,
pages 33 (above), 34 (John Wyclif), 35 (Jan
Hus), 41, 51 (below), 54-55 (below); British
Museum, pages 51 (above), 52 (right); Camera
Press, pages 21, 54-55 (above); Church
Missionary Society, page 64; Colorific!
pages 14-15; Czechoslovak Tourist Board,
pages 34-35; Keith Ellis Collection, page 53;
Sara Ellis, page 52 (left); Mary Evans Picture
Library, pages 54, 57; Susan Griggs Agency,
page 18; Sonia Halliday Photographs: F.H.C.
Birch, pages 30-31, Sonia Halliday, pages 2-3,
5 (Taurus Mts), 10, 11, 30; Alan Hutchison
Library, pages 25 (below), 56-57; Jesuit
Mission, pages 28-29; Keystone Press
Agency, pages 50-51; Lion Publishing: David
Alexander, pages 3, 4, 5, 10-11, 19, 24-25, 37
(below), Jon Willcocks, pages 18-19, 22-23
(all), 32, cover, endpapers & contents pages;
Mansell Collection, pages 7, 8-9
(Lauros-Giraudon), 33 (below), 34 (Thomas à
Kempis), 36 (both), 38, 39, 40, 40-41, 46,
60-61; Museo de San Marco/Bisonte, page 35
(Girolamo Savonarola); Novosti Press
Agency, pages 58-59; Open Doors with
Brother Andrew, page 63 (below);
Picturepoint, pages 14, 20, 44-45;
Popperfoto, pages 9, 16-17; Salvation Army,
page 61; Swiss National Tourist Office, pages
38-39; Tear Fund, pages 62, 63 (above)

Map on pages 6-7 by James Watson

Printed in Italy by New Interlitho S.P.A.,
Milan

CONTENTS

Parts of Nazareth have changed little since the time of Jesus.

THE FOUNDER OF CHRISTIANITY

*Born in obscurity, brought up in a poor family,
followed by scores of ordinary people, hounded to
death-by-crucifixion . . .*

It is about 4 BC; we are not sure of the exact date. A boy is born to Mary, a young woman from Nazareth. He is given the common enough name of Jesus. Mary's husband, Joseph, is an older man, a carpenter or local builder.

We are in the early years of the Roman Empire. Caesar Octavianus — later, and better, known as Augustus — is emperor. In Judea, Herod the Great is king. Roman 'procurators' rule the occupied Jewish nation.

We know almost nothing about Jesus' life over the next thirty years. But when he reached thirty he began to preach in the local Jewish meeting-place, the synagogue, in Nazareth. His challenging words were not appreciated by his neighbours: after all, he was only the local carpenter's son. In the cities of Judea, he was despised as a rural rabble-rouser. Three short years later he was degradingly executed at the Place of the Skull, just outside the capital city of Jerusalem.

From such small beginnings sprang a world-transforming movement.

Man with a message

When Jesus preached to his townspeople in the synagogue in Nazareth, he took a text which summed up his aims:

*'The Spirit of the Lord is upon me,
because he has anointed me to preach good news
to the poor.
He has sent me to proclaim release to the captives
and recovering of sight to the blind;
to set at liberty those who are oppressed,
to proclaim the acceptable year of the Lord.'*

Then he outraged his neighbours with the apparently blasphemous claim: 'Today this Scripture has been fulfilled in your hearing.'

The young man now set about gathering a group of twelve followers, nucleus of a new People of God to replace the old Twelve Tribes of Israel. His disciples were mostly ordinary tradespeople and craftsmen: fishermen, traders and tax-gatherers. Closest of his friends were Peter, James and John.

A new start

Together they started travelling the country, showing in words and actions what this new 'kingdom of God' was to be: not the deliverance of Israel from Roman oppression, but something much more breathtaking: a whole new start for people, a new birth, a way out of the vicious spiral of sin and death, a whole new creation, starting now but to be finalized in the future . . .

The people followed him everywhere, not only for his colourful teaching — he used stories from farming and everyday life as 'parables' to teach spiritual truths — but also for his healing. His love went out to them as he demonstrated the power of the new age. Cripples were cured, the insane made whole, even the dead raised. He showed too his power over nature: 'even the winds and waves obeyed him.'

But he was no mere wonder-worker. He avoided publicity. When his followers realized who he was, he told them to keep it to themselves. He did not want people to follow him for the wrong reasons.

Gathering storm

Inevitably, his radical teaching did not please everybody. The Jewish zealots, dedicated to overthrowing the Roman occupying forces, wanted violence, not love. The religious leaders, criticized by Jesus for reducing God's law to petty rules, attacked him in turn for going round with social outcasts — the tax-gatherers who were traitors to their country, the prostitutes, the religiously 'unclean'. 'It's the sick people who need the doctor, not those who are well,' Jesus retorted. His message of hope was for everyone, not just the people of Israel. It was more than they could stomach.

In the third year of his teaching, the religious leaders had had enough. Jesus was in Jerusalem for the Passover festival. It was the opportunity they wanted. He had to die.

JERUSALEM AD 30

'God has raised this very Jesus from death, and we are all witnesses to this fact.'
The apostle Peter

Jesus entered Jerusalem in triumph for his final Passover festival. He rode on the back of a donkey, and the crowds tore down palm-branches to cover the roadway, shouting, 'Hosanna! Blessed is he who comes in the name of the Lord.' The Jewish prophet Zechariah had predicted centuries earlier that their king would appear 'humble and riding on an ass' and would 'command peace to the nations'.

The following day, Jesus went into the temple. He was furious with the money-changers and salesmen who polluted the Holy Place by cheating the poor. He scattered them and overturned their tables.

Last Supper

Towards the end of the week, Jesus ate a solemn meal with his disciples in a hired room. He foretold that one of the twelve would betray him. Then he used the wine and bread to picture the meaning of his coming death. Just as the bread was broken, the wine poured out, so his body would be broken, his life-blood poured out for them. Just as they shared the bread and wine together, so they would share in his death. Jesus was to take their sinfulness, the evil and wrongdoing of a world gone rotten, down into death, once and for all . . .

Then they all went out of the city to a garden called Gethsemane, where Jesus was arrested. He had been betrayed by Judas Iscariot, one of the twelve.

Condemned

In the middle of the night, Jesus was hustled away for a hurried hearing. When he answered the high priest Caiaphas' question: 'Are you the Christ, the promised Deliverer?' with the words 'I am', this was enough to secure death for blasphemy.

But the Jews were powerless to carry out the capital sentence. So they took their prisoner to the Roman governor, Pilate: but Pilate could find no reason to punish him, and tried to reason with them. By this time an angry mob had gathered, incited by the religious leaders. It was enough to intimidate Pilate into sentencing Jesus to death on the cross.

Crucified

Jesus was forced to carry his cross out to the execution place — Golgotha — after being whipped by Roman soldiers; he died with convicted thieves crucified on either side; on his lips the words, 'Father, forgive . . .'

By late the same afternoon, Jesus' body had been laid in a rock-hewn tomb, the property of a rich Jew, and sealed up. The Romans set a guard, to avoid any trouble.

At this point in the laconic reporting of the Gospel records there is a pause, a moment of bated breath, the hush before dawn.

Jesus is alive!

For when some of Jesus' woman followers came to the tomb the following Sunday morning, they found it empty. not believing them, the others came to see for themselves: the graveclothes were there undisturbed, but the body had gone.

Then, not once but on numerous occasions, they met Jesus, risen from the dead. They met him in a room in Jerusalem and by the Lake of Galilee; others met him while travelling to a village west of Jerusalem; they met him in broad daylight when he was least expected; they ate with him — it was no ghost, no hallucination. At one point Jesus appeared to 500 followers.

This was the turning-point for the disciples. On the dismal night of his death, it seemed as if the story was finished. In truth, it was. A whole world had come to an end.

But now they were new men. They had complete conviction that Jesus had risen from the dead. And not only that, it was the seal on Jesus' claim that could now be made public. He was none other than God himself, the promised Deliverer of his people, of those who put their trust in him. The Spirit of God himself came to fill them with new life and the urgency of the new-found good news.

'They found the stone rolled away from the entrance to the tomb, so they went in; but they did not find the body of the Lord Jesus', Luke reported. The fact that Jesus had come alive from the dead transformed the first disciples. The resurrection of Jesus has been the core of the Christian message ever since.

The church is born

Peter was the first to speak out — a call to believe in Jesus, crucified, risen, and now at God's right hand. Those entering the new society of believers should be baptized, and would know the coming of the Holy Spirit for themselves.

The early, heady days were marked by many conversions. The believers celebrated their faith together in a common meal, a love feast and thanksgiving celebration which echoed that last supper with Jesus. They experimented with communal property and shared possessions.

But the Jewish religious leaders quickly clamped down. Believers were thrown into prison. Stephen, an outspoken Christian leader, was stoned to death.

Despite opposition, new converts continued enthusiastically; they began to fan out from Jerusalem, taking their faith with them.

PAUL: MISSIONARY EXTRAORDINARY

The conversion of Saul of Tarsus gave the early Christian church a giant of a leader and a tireless campaigner.

For sheer vitality, breadth of vision, intellectual and spiritual vigour, Saul of Tarsus is unequalled. His ambition was to take the message of Christ to the whole of the ancient world. He wrote numerous letters to encourage and instruct the first Christians. He broke down barriers of prejudice, discovering that in Christ there was no distinction between Jew and Gentile, between slave and freedman, between man and woman.

Saul was born into a strict Jewish family, with Roman citizenship, in Tarsus, in what is today south-eastern Turkey. He became a 'Hebrew of the Hebrews', and a furious opponent of the new sect following Jesus.

About-turn

In about AD 33 Saul set off to Damascus to suppress the new group of Christians there. But on the way he was blinded by a vision, and heard a voice saying: 'I am Jesus, whom you are persecuting.' The humbled zealot made an about-turn, and now poured all his energies into serving Christ.

Paul — to use his Roman name — retired for three years to Arabia, re-emerging afire with his new mission. He was determined to preach to both Jew and non-Jew — an idea that was unacceptable at first to many of the Jewish believers in Jerusalem. He preached first in Damascus, and then moved to Tarsus.

On the road again

But it was from Antioch, where believers were first called 'Christians', that Paul set out, with Barnabas and John Mark, on his first missionary journey. They travelled first to Cyprus, then into Asia Minor (modern Turkey), where Mark left them. Paul's method was to start in the synagogue, but never to conceal his purpose of converting non-Jews too.

After their first, difficult, journey, the two returned to Antioch. There followed a Council in Jerusalem, where the issue of the mission to non-Jews was debated.

Into Europe

Paul next set out on a second journey. He re-visited the towns of Asia Minor, buttressing

A flourishing Christian church was established at Corinth, a prosperous centre of trade and industry.

As a Roman citizen, Paul enjoyed special privileges. As a prisoner, he asked to be taken to Rome to be tried before the emperor. But there, in the capital of the empire, he was probably martyred.

Paul's first landfall in Europe was Neapolis, the port for Philippi.

the faith of the new converts. At Lystra he was joined by the young Timothy, who helped him in the province of Galatia. From Troas, Paul responded to a dream-message by crossing into Europe with the gospel. His message won followers in Philippi and along the Roman road towards Athens, the cultural capital of the Hellenistic Mediterranean world. There he confronted sophisticated paganism and met with derision — but some believed.

Paul settled nearby in Corinth for eighteen months, and it was probably from here that he began to write the letters to churches he knew, which now form part of our New Testament. After a third journey and two years in Ephesus, Paul returned to Jerusalem, taking with him a collection to relieve hardship among the Christians there.

Shipwreck

While in Jerusalem, Paul's Pharisee enemies took the opportunity to have him imprisoned. Making a virtue of his misfortune, Paul appealed to Caesar, and was eventually transported to Rome for his appeal to be heard. Despite shipwreck on Malta, Paul finally arrived in Rome, where Christianity had already taken root. He remained a prisoner there for two years, and possibly at some time travelled to Spain with the gospel. He was apparently executed during the persecution instigated by the infamous Emperor Nero.

LETTERS TO YOUNG CHURCHES

Paul is known to us not only through the vivid historical writing of Luke in the book of Acts, but also in the numerous letters he himself penned to the scattered churches he had founded throughout the Mediterranean world.

Paul's letter to the **Romans** is his most thorough explanation of his message: we are all, Jews and non-Jews alike, cut off from God because of our sinful nature; it is by trusting Jesus and his death for our sinfulness that we can be 'made just' in God's sight and live the new life of the Spirit. In **Galatians**, too, Paul anxiously urges the new believers to hold on to their freedom in Christ, not go back to the slavery of Jewish legalism.

In the two letters to the **Corinthians** we see Paul both as pastor and theologian, helping a church in the midst of a pagan seaport sort out questions of life and behaviour, of spiritual gifts and above all of Christian love.

A recurring theme in Paul's letters, notably in **Ephesians** and **Colossians**, is the greatness, the sheer cosmic dimension, of Christ's person and work. The new era he came to announce, and make possible by his own death and resurrection, is a totally new creation. As Paul explains to the **Philippians**, it has enormous implications for how we should live now.

For, one day, Jesus will return to complete the salvation he has started. Right from the start, in his letters to the **Thessalonians**, Paul looked to the day when the new age would be fulfilled.

As an older man, Paul wrote to his young travelling companion **Timothy**, and to **Titus**. Full of wise advice for the young Christians, Paul was burdened with the care of the churches to the last.

Paul's preaching was so successful in Ephesus that local silversmiths, afraid of lost sales of statues of the goddess Diana, raised a riot. The citizens gathered to protest at the theatre, which held over 25,000 people.

Paul's missionary journeys involved long overland treks, including the dangerous pass through the Taurus mountains in what is now Turkey.

CHRISTIANITY EXPANDS

Peter and Paul both died at the hands of the executioner. But the task they began was continued by others. By the end of the first century, the church had spread widely across the Mediterranean world.

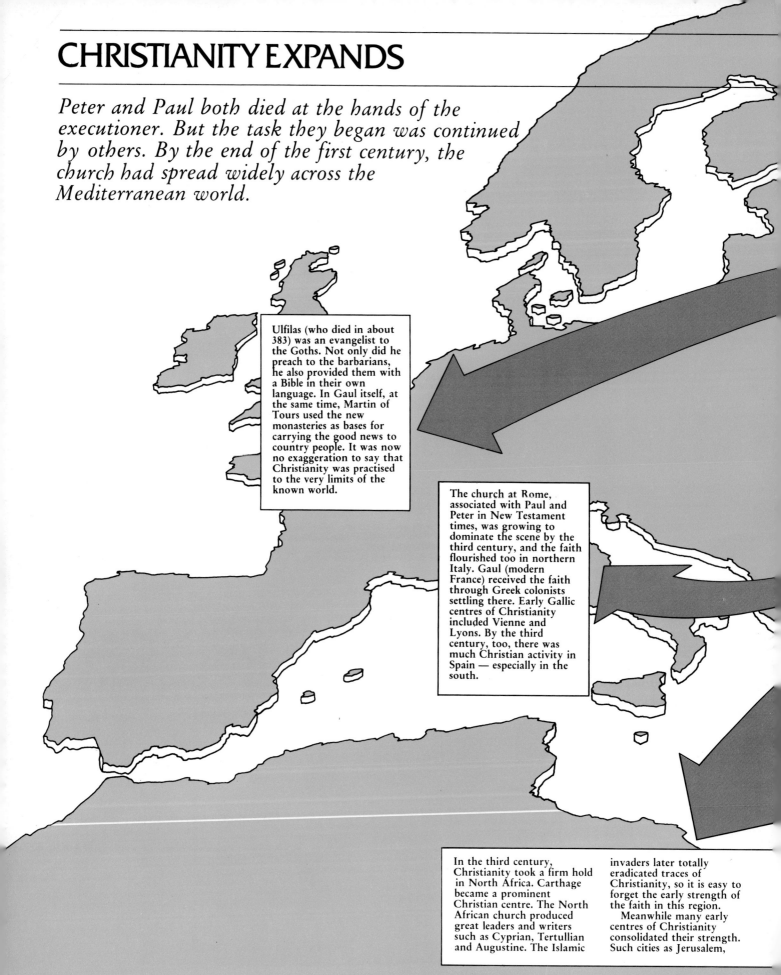

Ulfilas (who died in about 383) was an evangelist to the Goths. Not only did he preach to the barbarians, he also provided them with a Bible in their own language. In Gaul itself, at the same time, Martin of Tours used the new monasteries as bases for carrying the good news to country people. It was now no exaggeration to say that Christianity was practised to the very limits of the known world.

The church at Rome, associated with Paul and Peter in New Testament times, was growing to dominate the scene by the third century, and the faith flourished too in northern Italy. Gaul (modern France) received the faith through Greek colonists settling there. Early Gallic centres of Christianity included Vienne and Lyons. By the third century, too, there was much Christian activity in Spain — especially in the south.

In the third century, Christianity took a firm hold in North Africa. Carthage became a prominent Christian centre. The North African church produced great leaders and writers such as Cyprian, Tertullian and Augustine. The Islamic invaders later totally eradicated traces of Christianity, so it is easy to forget the early strength of the faith in this region.

Meanwhile many early centres of Christianity consolidated their strength. Such cities as Jerusalem,

Jesus' description of himself as the 'good shepherd, who is willing to die for the sheep' inspired the design on this third-century Christian coffin, which also features a man studying sacred texts and a woman praying.

Christianity was not confined within the boundaries of the empire. Tradition has it that the apostle Thomas extended the mission to India, and founded the church there. By the third century, there were Christians in Arabia, and widespread conversions in Armenia followed later in the century. By converting King Tiridates, the aristocratic missionary Gregory the Illuminator christianized his nation.

The first expansion had been from Jerusalem to Caesarea and Joppa. Then Christians moved to Samaria and Syria. Next came Paul's pioneering journeys into Asia Minor and Greece. The gospel reached Rome.

By the second century, Jewish Christianity was dwindling. Jewish Christians in Jerusalem had already suffered severe persecution; James, brother of John, was martyred in about AD 44.

Antioch and Corinth continued to be influential. Missionaries took the faith to new areas within the empire. Outstanding men such as Gregory the Wonderworker (died about 270) won fresh converts from paganism.

In its second century, Christianity crossed the Mediterranean from Italy into the Roman province of North Africa and, later in the century, into Egypt. Meanwhile, the previous Christian gains were consolidated, as Christianity spread from its urban strongholds to the surrounding countryside.

THE BLOOD OF THE MARTYRS

'Eighty-six years I have served him, and he has done me no wrong. How can I then blaspheme my king who saved me?'
Polycarp

The first centuries of Christianity were not a triumphant story of continuous, unimpeded expansion. We have only to mention the name Nero and the black shadow of persecution enters. Nero, the petulant egoist, blamed Christians for the disastrous fire in Rome in July AD 64. A Roman historian wrote:

'Nero set up as the culprits and punished with the utmost cruelty a class hated for their abominations, commonly called Christians . . . Besides being put to death, they were made objects of entertainment. They were clothed in the skins of beasts and torn to death by dogs; others were crucified . . .'

Anti-Christian graffiti scratched on a Roman wall depicted a boy raising his hand in worship in front of a crucified figure with an ass's head. The words scribbled underneath read: 'Alexamenus worships his god.'

Faith in suffering

But this infamous episode, though possibly the most spectacular, was neither the first nor the last example of persecution of Christians. Both Jews and Romans oppressed believers in Palestine; and persecution in Rome continued intermittently for the next three centuries. The Emperor Domitian (–96), for instance, included Christians among the victims of his displeasure. Insecure emperors such as Valerianus and Decius used persecution to draw attention away from their own failures.

Christians were hated for a variety of reasons. They were said to be atheists, since they would not take part in emperor-worship. They were accused of obscene worship-practices — the eucharistic words 'eating Christ's flesh' were taken as evidence of cannibalism. And they were held to be disloyal to the state, since they claimed a prior loyalty to God.

The last sustained persecution came under Diocletian (284-305). After this, things changed dramatically. The Emperor Galerius announced that Christianity was to be officially tolerated. Constantine gave Christians religious freedom — and later adopted their faith himself.

Gladiators' fights and mock naval battles were staged in Rome's famous amphitheatre, the Colosseum. Prisoners, sometimes Christians, were thrown to lions and bears in the arena for the spectators' amusement.

DEFENDERS OF THE FAITH

Some Christian writers attempted to justify their faith to their opponents by writing reasoned arguments for what they believed. One such writer was Justin Martyr, who came to Christianity as a well-read pagan philosopher. He set out to show that Christianity need not challenge political leaders, and that it could carry on a dialogue with other beliefs and schools of thought. Despite this, Justin paid for his beliefs with his life, being executed under the Emperor Marcus Aurelius in 165.

A later defender of Christianity, Tertullian, was more forthright and effective than Justin. He abandoned attempts at bridge-building: 'What is there in common between Athens and Jerusalem?' he demanded. He coined the unforgettable phrase, 'The martyr's blood is the seed of the church.' But he himself survived to die naturally.

Janani Luwum, Archbishop of Uganda, died in February 1977. Described by Idi Amin's government as 'a traffic accident', his death was widely believed to be the deliberate silencing by Amin of an outstanding Christian leader.

Pressure and persecution

But persecution continued down the centuries. The Muslim invaders of North Africa swiftly removed all traces of the faith. In later centuries, peoples evangelized by Christian missionaries often expressed their anger at such activities by violent rebellion. The Japanese cruelly undid the work of seventeenth-century Jesuit missionaries; the Communist Chinese attempted to uproot Christianity in their efforts to erase 'bourgeois imperialist' culture from their country. Dictators such as Hitler and Amin have used the bloodiest of methods to remove stubborn Christians who dared resist their tyranny.

At the martyrdom of Polycarp

The Proconsul urged him and said, 'Swear, and I will release you; curse the Christ.'

And Polycarp said, 'Eighty-six years I have served him, and he has done me no wrong. How can I then blaspheme my king who saved me?'

GOD AND CAESAR

From being the religion of a despised and persecuted minority, Christianity under Emperor Constantine gained official acceptance. But recognition brought its own dangers . . .

The Roman Empire was torn with disorder in the third century, and only finally recovered stability under Constantine the Great. As a young military commander, Constantine worshipped the sun. But while marching south through Italy he claimed he had a vision of the Christian 'Chi Rho' sign across the face of the sun, with the message: 'In this sign you will conquer.' With this encouragement, he went on to capture Rome and control the empire; in gratitude he declared his allegiance to the Christian God.

From persecution to privilege

With this radical turn-about, Christianity emerged from centuries of oppression to become a favoured religion. But now came the temptations of position and recognition, of power and riches. Constantine created a Christian empire, and with it changed the whole concept of the faith.

Christian places of worship were now for the first time officially permitted. Christian clergy, like pagan priests, were exempted from civic duties. The first day of the week (still called 'Sun'-day) was a holy day. Crucifixion was abolished.

But Constantine did not make Christianity the state religion; it was far from being the faith of the majority of his subjects. He gave it official recognition, and probably hoped it would help weld together his unwieldy empire.

Christians now found themselves with unhoped-for privileges. They hailed Constantine as God's chosen leader. Eusebius, an early historian of the church, claimed the empire was designed by God for the salvation of humanity. Christians realized that Rome and its empire were now theirs.

Constantine's city

But Constantine went on to take other far-reaching decisions. He gave the empire a new capital: Constantinople, Constantine's own city. He built it at the strategic point where Asia and Europe almost touch, on the narrow neck of the Bosphorus.

Built by Justinian, the huge cathedral of St Sophia was completed in 537. It became a mosque in 1453 after the Turkish conquest, and is now a museum. This richly-decorated domed basilica is one of the finest examples of Byzantine architecture.

Modern-day Istanbul, formerly Constantinople, bustles with life on the site chosen by Constantine in AD 330 for his capital of the eastern half of the Roman Empire.

The old town on this site was called Byzantium — hence the term Byzantine for its culture. In 1930 the Turks re-named it Istanbul. Here Constantine created a great cathedral church, named Santa Sophia. It was destroyed by fire in the sixth century, but replaced by the present unforgettable structure.

Christianity was now part of the fabric of the empire. It helped a man's promotion prospects in the imperial service to be a Christian. Tax concessions and military service privileges were offered to believers. Later, the Emperor Theodosius penalized non-Christians with similar laws to those once enforced against Christians.

Power — and problems

The emperor was well aware of his own status in the Christian hierarchy. Great mosaics celebrated the emperor's power; he often featured prominently as God's first representative on earth. Such resplendent mosaics have survived intact at Ravenna, on the coast of Italy, which rose to importance as the chief port on the route between Rome and Constantinople. The Emperor Justinian is portrayed as Ruler of the Universe, just below Christ, Ruler of Everything; beside him is the bishop, Maxentius, content to act as the emperor's servant.

However, some churchmen refused to kow-tow. When the Emperor Theodosius massacred 5,000 citizens for rioting, the bishop of Milan, Ambrose, insisted that he should do public penance. He threatened to ban him from communion until he complied — excommunication was a weapon which the medieval church was frequently to wield.

The official adoption of Christianity had other, grave, consequences. Christ's appeal to the meek and humble was often substituted by a new allurement for the social climber. The evil of slavery, rife in the Roman Empire, was now safe from attack by Christians. The emperors could not keep their meddling fingers out of church affairs — Constantine himself tried to dictate over complex areas of doctrine at the Council of Nicaea in 325.

The son of a peasant, Justinian rose to become the last emperor to rule in the West (527-565). He was obsessed with the ideal of the Roman Empire and worked tirelessly to restore its former glories.

WHAT DO WE BELIEVE?

Christian belief is based on the truth of the Bible. But how did that Bible come together? And what happened when its authority was challenged?

As questions arose about Christian belief and practice, believers learned how to live out their faith in the context of everyday life.

As the churches came into existence, Christians began to ask questions about their faith. What exactly did Jesus do and say? How should they celebrate the Lord's Supper? Who was to lead the church? What should they do if church members sinned publicly?

As long as the apostles were living, such questions could be referred to them. They were always ready to retell the teachings and acts of Jesus. But as they died, it became vital to have a more permanent record of such teachings.

The making of the Bible

One obvious collection of writings to provide a key to Christ's life was the Jewish Old Testament. By the end of the first century AD the contents of the Old Testament were fixed as including those sixty-six books which are now universally accepted. A few other books were accepted by some; known as the Deutero-canonical books they are accepted as of lesser authority by some Christian churches today.

When it came to more recent writings, it was clear that Paul's letters and the four Gospels were foundation documents. Being by apostles they contained firsthand knowledge and experience of Jesus. Other writings proved more controversial; there were arguments over the letters of Jude, John and Peter, over Hebrews, James and the Revelation. Some churches held that other writings were good enough to be bracketed with the apostles' writings — for example, 'The

CREEDS AND COUNCILS

Over the years, core-statements summing up basic Christianity began to emerge. They probably evolved as part of the baptismal or other services, when a summary was used to outline the beliefs of a new convert.

Gradually the early leaders of the church added to, or explained, these brief statements, three third-century Christian leaders in particular:

Irenaeus came from Lyons in Gaul, present-day France. He spent much of his time defending the faith against heresies such as Gnosticism. But he was careful always to base his arguments soundly in biblical teaching, and illuminated afresh the central beliefs of the church.

Tertullian, by contrast, came from Carthage in North Africa. He was trained as a lawyer, and could present a clear defence of his beliefs. He would

have nothing to do with earlier attempts to make Christianity fit in with Greek philosophy; for him one of the glories of the faith was its uniqueness.

Origen came from a third Christian centre, Alexandria, where Greek thinking rivalled Christianity. He was a giant among intellectuals, and largely responsible for introducing new thought-forms to express Christian beliefs.

After this trio of thinkers, came a series of Church Councils, with the stupendous task of expressing clearly two basic paradoxes of the Christian faith:

● There is one God — yet God has revealed himself as Father, Son and Holy Spirit.

● Christ has both a divine and a human nature. He is both God and man.

Not surprisingly, it took a number of meetings, and much debate, to come to

Shepherd of Hermas' and 'The Letter of Barnabas'.

But eventually the list of New Testament books emerged as we know it. We have no record of it before AD 369, but it represented a consensus of the writings whose authority stood out from the rest. They helped clarify the doctrines of the church, made plain the way of salvation, and all had proven links with the name of an apostle.

Basic beliefs threatened

The Christians were anxious to agree the books of the New Testament because unorthodox beliefs were springing up to compete with the orthodox faith. For example, the Gnostics claimed to have a secret 'knowledge'; they did not need the literal, history-based beliefs of ordinary Christians. They rejected the Old Testament — or treated it as a mere allegory. They picked up ideas from various religions,

Alexandria was a major centre of Greek or 'Hellenistic' culture and philosophy. It was here that the Old Testament was first translated from Hebrew into Greek. Christian scholars in Alexandria tried to express the new faith in terms of Greek thinking.

anything like a satisfactory conclusion. Councils met at Nicaea, Constantinople, Ephesus and Chalcedon between 325 and 451, grappling with the complex questions. But the debate was vital: Christianity depended both on right living and on right teaching. The beliefs expressed must reflect the truth.

Critics have often pointed out that the Trinity, as such, is never referred to in the Bible. Perhaps the most outspoken critic in those early days was Arius, who taught that the Son was subordinate to the Father. His opinions were debated — and eventually rejected — at Nicaea. The party of Athanasius later came up with what has become the orthodox statement:

'We believe in one Lord Jesus Christ, the Son of God, begotten of the Father, only-begotten, that is, of the substance of the Father, God of God, Light of Light, true God of true God, begotten not made, of one substance with the Father, through whom all things were made . . .'

The second problem was how to say at one and the same time that Jesus was fully man — the figure from the Gospels who suffered, wept and died — and fully God. This, too, provoked great debate and accusations of heresy, but finally they came up with a long, but precise, statement at the Council of Chalcedon (451), claiming Christ to be:

'one and the same . . . Son, Lord, Only-begotten, to be acknowledged in two natures without confusion, without change, without division, or without separation.'

With such statements of belief, the church was strong to resist the onslaughts of opponents who ridiculed such apparent complexities.

claiming to be higher and more spiritual than the rest.

Several New Testament books attack such beliefs, which forced Christians to define carefully what they really did believe.

Another threat to orthodox beliefs came from Marcion, son of a bishop. He regarded the created world as evil: full of fleas, flies and fever! Marcion rejected the Old Testament together with any New Testament books that smacked of the God of the Law. He tried to reduce the sacred writings to those which spoke only of the God of love, the God of salvation.

THE BISHOP OF ROME

The Holy Roman Empire dominated medieval politics, society, literature.

Many debates have centred on the leadership of the church. In New Testament times 'elder', 'presbyter' and 'bishop' were names used interchangeably for the leaders of the local church. 'Deacons' were appointed to help serve its needs.

As the church became more of an institution, the bishop emerged as a leading figure, with responsibility for an area rather than one local church. And in due course the bishop of Rome became 'first among equals'.

Papal prestige

An early list tried to demonstrate that the bishop of Rome was in direct line from Peter, claimed as the city's first bishop. The bishops of Rome began claiming the right to intervene in local disputes, and to lead the increasingly centralized church.

With Constantine's conversion, the bishop of Rome received new honours. The emperor constructed a great basilica over the shrine of St Peter on the Vatican Hill — replaced in the sixteenth century by the St Peter's we now know. Constantine also built a church over St Paul's shrine on the Ostian Way, and presented the bishop with the Lateran Palace as an official residence.

But the Roman Empire was in its death-throes. In 410 Alaric sacked Rome, which had been secure from invasion for 800 years. 'The city which has taken the whole world is itself taken.' Waves of barbarian invaders swept through Italy, until in 476 the last emperor in the West, Romulus Augustulus, was deposed.

But the bishops of Rome continued their claims to supreme power. Sometimes they were backed by emperors desperate for support. Leo I claimed that, as Peter's successor, the pope possessed the apostle's authority. Pope Gregory the Great wielded his authority effectively by taking civil and military control when Rome was threatened by Lombard invaders at the end of the sixth century; but he did not neglect his spiritual duties, and sent a mission to Britain, for example.

The power game

But time and again pope and emperor locked in combat to try their strength. A temporary truce came in 800, when Pope Leo III crowned

Marble, mosaic, gilt and bronze enrich the interior of St Peter's Basilica in Rome — the world's largest church. The pope is spiritual leader of the Roman Catholic church, the largest Christian community in the world.

Charlemagne emperor. The new emperor stimulated a renewal of learning, impressive enough to be labelled the 'Carolingian Renaissance'. But peace was short-lived; Pope Gregory VII, and above all Innocent III (1198-1216), were militantly jealous of the church's rights. Innocent it was who tried to pull England's King John into line with the weapon of excommunication.

But with Pope Boniface VIII, claims far outreached power; he languished as prisoner of King Philip IV of France. Yet the popes continued to lay claim to supreme authority — while weakening their reputation for holiness by entangling themselves in power politics. The pope was increasingly criticized — even the spiritual weapon of excommunication was dirtied by excessive and inappropriate use. The greed of the popes for taxes, tithes and tolls scandalized Europe.

Reform

There were, of course, attempts at reform. In the fifteenth century much hope was vainly invested in a series of Church Councils. Even the personal holiness and humanist learning of a pope such as Nicholas V (1447-1455) was cancelled out by his infamous successors. Later Renaissance popes were more noted for their paganism, nepotism, immorality and Machiavellian politics. Probably the greatest damage was inflicted by Rodrigo Borgia (-1503), uniquely unfitted for the supreme position in the church.

The concept of a 'Holy Roman Empire' was to take a long time to die. It dominated medieval politics, society, literature. Reformers and leaders of protest movements such as Jan Hus in Bohemia, who tried to return to the doctrines and church of the New Testament, found they were up against the might of an empire, and their cause became inextricably entwined with local nationalism.

Since the break-up of the Holy Roman Empire, the papacy has of course had to adjust. At times it has tried to re-emphasize its authority, as in the last century. In our present century, however, particularly following the Vatican II Council of 1962-65, it is seeking again the role of leadership of a 'church in the world', of service rather than imperialism.

A YEAR IN THE LIFE OF THE CHURCH

*Just as families mark birthdays and anniversaries,
so the Christian church developed its own calendar
of special seasons of celebration.*

There is a natural cycle for all living things. Day follows night. Summer follows spring. Such patterns are reflected in many religious rituals and traditions. Christians accepted this, and often adapted pagan festivals for themselves. Events in the life of Christ, and anniversaries in the church's life, are celebrated at set times in the year. As varied traditions grew up in different parts of the church, different dates or contrasting celebrations evolved.

Easter

From the beginning, Easter has been the most important annual Christian festival. At first, it was often called the Christian Passover, coinciding with the Jewish Passover, and symbolizing God's salvation through Christ's sacrifice. It was the time for specially remembering Christ's death and celebrating his resurrection.

As early as the second century, there were great discussions about the right date to celebrate Easter. Some churches preferred to keep to the Jewish calendar, while others used a different dating system. The Western churches finally agreed on a date for Easter at the Synod of Whitby in 664.

At first, Easter was only a one-day festival, marking both Jesus' death and his resurrection. As pilgrims began to spend the festival in the Holy Land, they retraced Jesus' steps during his final week in Jerusalem, and a complicated series of Easter services was introduced to mark the various events. So, by the fourth century, Palm Sunday, Maundy Thursday, Good Friday and Easter Sunday were all celebrated in special ways.

At the same time, it became customary for those wanting to be baptized to be prepared during the forty days of 'Lent' (marking Jesus' period of preparation in the wilderness), leading up to Easter.

But the celebrations did not finish on Easter Day. The seven weeks following culminated in the celebration of the giving of the Holy Spirit on the Day of Pentecost, after the celebration of Jesus' ascension.

Christmas

The other major fixed point in the Christian year was Christmas, celebrating Jesus' birth in

In many parts of the world, the events of the first Easter — the death and rising again of Jesus — are celebrated with colourful processions and tableaux.

THE TRAPPINGS OF RELIGION

The growth of the church calendar illustrates the development of Christianity from being a movement with few trappings to a more formalized 'religion'.

In the early days a local church had several leaders, and the ministry was shared among those of different gifts. Before the eucharist ('thanksgiving') or communion acquired the idea of sacrifice, there was no thought of priesthood: Christ was both priest, representing us to God, and sacrifice, dying on our behalf. So there was no distinction between 'clergy' and 'laity'.

With the development of a priesthood came increased religious observances. Masses were said on behalf of the dead, chapels and institutions set up by those wealthy enough (and fearful enough of purgatory) to endow them. The veneration of local saints became superstitious, almost a pagan ritual to appease the spirits. So saints' days took on great importance.

The person of Jesus, too, became remote from ordinary people. He was depicted as Christ in glory and grandeur. Increasingly people turned to the Virgin Mary as one who would sympathize with their afflictions and speak to God on their behalf.

Today many are learning afresh that Jesus was man as well as God. In rediscovering the Bible, they are rediscovering the message of the New Testament: 'because he himself has suffered and been tempted, he is able to help those who are tempted.'

Bethlehem. Christians observed Christmas on various dates, at least as early as the fourth century. In the West, most churches fixed Christmas as 25 December; in the East, 6 January was the chosen date. Probably both dates were previously pagan holidays. In the fifth century, the churches of East and West agreed that 25 December would mark Jesus' birthday, 6 January the coming of the wise men to the baby Jesus (Epiphany).

Just as Easter had its preparatory period, Christmas was led up to by the season of Advent, when Christians looked forward to Jesus' second coming.

High days and holidays

By AD 600, many minor festivals had appeared in the Christian calendar — for example, saints' days for such figures as Stephen, James and John, and Holy Innocents' day, marking Herod's massacre of the baby boys in Judea. Now the Virgin Mary and local saints and martyrs were all allocated their own days. The Celtic church even added All Saints' Day.

But the church calendar, the seasons of Easter and Christmas, had a practical purpose, too. The high days and holidays were times of great celebration. But in between the calendar was the framework for the church's teaching. The 'lectionary', or scheme of Bible readings, was designed to take people through the Bible's teaching over the course of the year.

THE LORD'S SUPPER

'Then Jesus took a piece of bread, gave thanks to God, broke it, and gave it to them . . .'

Enemies accused the first Christians of cannibalism. They called them a gang of desperadoes formed of the lowest dregs of the population, ignorant men and women who attended nocturnal gatherings, solemn feasts and barbarous meals.

These accusations were based on a total misunderstanding of the central focus of early Christian meetings: when bread and wine were shared as Christ's 'flesh' and 'blood'.

A shared meal

At first the eucharist was a common meal, in the course of which bread and wine were shared as a vivid reminder of the death and resurrection of Jesus and of the believers' 'sharing' in it: they had died to sin in Jesus' death, and in his resurrection they had been raised to newness of life.

Gradually the Western church put more and more emphasis on the act of celebrating the eucharist, or 'mass', and on the power that was believed to spring from this 're-enacting' of Jesus' sacrifice of himself upon the cross.

Midnight mass is celebrated at the Church of the Nativity in Bethlehem.

In time, popes began to threaten obstinate rulers with exclusion from the eucharist — a powerful sanction, with its threat of exclusion from heaven. Priests used similar persuasion with their wayward flocks. People started to attach magical significance to the bread and wine. Ordinary Christians were barred as unfit to drink the wine.

The Fourth Lateran Council proclaimed in 1215: 'The Body and Blood are truly contained in the Sacrament . . . under the appearance of bread and wine, after the bread has been changed into the Body, and the wine into the Blood, through the power of God.'

The reformers

Such views of the eucharist were later to be rejected by the reformers of the sixteenth century. Martin Luther demanded that believers should be offered

The Swiss Reformation leader Zwingli emphasized the fact that the communion is a remembrance of Jesus' death.

Bread and wine are the elements of the Christian communion, or eucharist: the broken bread depicting the body of Jesus, the wine his blood poured out for human sin.

both bread and wine; he rejected the idea that the bread and wine became Christ's body and blood. They benefited those who accepted them in faith, but the act of taking them in itself conveyed no mechanical blessing. Calvin, like Luther, believed the Lord's Supper to be an especially dramatic point in the Christian's communion with God.

But Luther's contemporary, the Swiss reformer Zwingli, went further. When he met Luther in dispute, the obstinate German pulled out a piece of chalk and scrawled on the table, 'This is my body'; that said it all. But for Zwingli the Lord's Supper was solely a sign, a metaphor: 'This is my body' meant 'This stands for my body'. For him, a vital part of the meal was its bringing together of fellow Christians in communion. It is this tradition which many of the Protestant denominations have taken up.

The apostle Paul gave Christians clear instructions for the celebration of the thanksgiving meal or 'eucharist', the 'Lord's Supper':

'For I received from the Lord what I also delivered to you, that the Lord Jesus on the night when he was betrayed took bread, and when he had given thanks, he broke it, and said, "This is my body which is for you. Do this in remembrance of me." In the same way also the cup, after supper, saying, "This cup is the new covenant in my blood. Do this, as often as you drink it, in remembrance of me." For as often as you eat this bread and drink the cup, you proclaim the Lord's death until he comes.'

THE EASTERN CHURCH

With their differing emphases, the Eastern and Western wings of the church gradually grew further apart: the Eastern church developing its own traditions of spirituality, worship and church life.

But this is not the whole story . . .

From the time of the Council of Chalcedon two traditions were developing, one centred on Rome, the other on Constantinople. Christians in the West are inclined to misunderstand or forget the Eastern Church, with its long, continuous story.

The Eastern Church never attempted to become independent of the state; it was in a way the spiritual arm of the state. The pattern was set by Constantine, who chaired the Council of Nicaea, guaranteeing the church's unity at the price of its independence. The emperors continued to work for peace and unity by overawing and directing the church. The bishop of Constantinople was rather like the emperor's court-preacher, and had always to curry favour. Those who, like John Chrysostom, criticized the emperor, were liable to be punished — as he was by execution.

Threats

As East and West drew apart, so did their answers to theological problems. In the East, debates about the nature of Christ particularly emphasized his divine side. The abstruse debates are slightly lightened by the quaint names of some of the participants — for example, Timothy the Cat and Peter the Fuller.

The Eastern Church faced a threat much more severe than the West. After the return of Muhammad to Mecca in 622, Islam exploded into a holy crusade of monotheism. Under the leadership of Abu Bakr, Islamic forces swept through the east. Egypt, Syria, Palestine and many Mediterranean islands were engulfed. The Eastern Church was drastically cut back, whereas the West only felt the impact when the Muslims swept along the North African coast, wiping out the former strongholds of North African Christianity.

Ikons

The East contrasted visually with Rome in its glory of images and representations of God. Such images had been frowned on in the West; Byzantium luxuriated in ikons of gold-leaf and extravagant colours: symbolic representations of Christ, his mother and the saints. These images were used to help the faithful to worship, and to

Ikons are pictures used in the Orthodox church as an aid to worshippers. But it is a short step from worshipping a spiritual being to worshipping the picture itself. Superstitious people in early Byzantine society began to believe that ikons had lives of their own.

express the mystery of holiness.

But even in the East, ikons provoked controversy. Possibly the Islamic ban on pictures of God filtered through. The Emperor Leo III raged against images, and fought to destroy them, though opposed by his monasteries. He was out-argued by John of Damascus (–749), but persisted in the struggle. Eventually, the ikon triumphed, and has continued inseparable from Eastern Christianity.

Parting of the ways

Other theological complexities divided East from West — and there was no love lost between their leaders. When the immovable Pope Leo IX wrote to the uncompromising Michael Cerularius in these words in 1054, there could only be one result:

'In prejudging the highest See, the see on which no judgment may be passed by any men, you have received anathema from all the Fathers of all the Venerable Councils.'

The unity of the church was finally severed.

Spirituality

In our own twentieth century, the renewed contact made possible by modern communications has opened the way again for renewed fellowship. The Western churches are learning from the spirituality and devotion of the Eastern traditions.

Churches in the East, such as the Russian Orthodox and the Coptic church in Egypt, are learning afresh how to live as a minority within society rather than being in a position of domination and power.

THE MONKS

Throughout Christian history there have been individuals and communities whose devotion to God and pursuit of holy living have led them to radical changes in life-style.

Some people have seen John the Baptizer and Jesus as contrasting personalities: the ascetic and the life-affirming. Both emphases have continued down through the story of Christianity.

In a cave in a crumbling cliff in the deserts of Egypt lived one of the earliest Christian monks: Antony (about 251–356). He went there to protest against the extravagances of 'fashionable' Christianity. He and his followers wanted to copy Jesus' example of struggling with the devil and his temptations in the desert.

Some of these early hermits felt their life was still not harsh enough, and decided to live on the tops of pillars. The most famous of these was Simeon Stylites, who spent his last twenty years atop such a pillar. Soon crowds of curious onlookers were flocking to stare at the spectacle.

New patterns

But it was when the desert hermits began to organize a form of group life that a new pattern of religious institution emerged. Just beneath Antony's cave stands a fifteen-centuries-old monastery, a stronghold against the devil. A group of monks agreed to live there under a common 'rule', though still maintaining solitariness.

Pachomius launched a different type of monasticism: he built a monastery on the banks of the Nile in the fourth century. Monks lived a communal existence, cultivating holiness.

Gradually such men as Jerome, Basil and Martin of Tours refined monastic ideals, with the basic call to personal holiness and withdrawal from the world and its temptations. Monasteries began to appear all around the Mediterranean, and took a firm hold in the West — one centre of early monasticism was in the Celtic west.

Labour and prayer

But of broader influence was Benedict of Nursia, who in the sixth century founded the Benedictine Order at Monte Cassino, in central Italy. His new rule and pattern spread fast, with its emphasis on service in holiness to God, rather than merely a harsh life-style. The abbot was spiritual father of the community; when a monk was accepted into the family, he had to remain

Reform

there for the rest of his life. His days were divided between labour, prayer, meals and sleep. Mass was celebrated on Sundays and holy days. Reading and writing were encouraged, and scholarship cultivated.

But in time monastic practice fell into disrepute, and monks became notorious for their immorality, their involvement in matters of state, and their intrigues.

But countless reform movements stemmed the decay. One centre of reform was the abbey of Cluny in central France. A succession of great abbots directed their brothers into greater devotion, and more disciplined worship, at the expense of physical work. The reforms soon spread, bringing new holiness and vitality. In England, for example, Dunstan reasserted the basics of Benedict's Rule.

The twelfth century saw a peak of reform, and many new monastic orders. The Carthusians, founded at Grande Chartreuse in 1084, re-emphasized withdrawal and the solitary holy life; the Cistercians, founded at Citeaux in 1098, recalled monks to simplicity. Their monastic houses were sited in barren country. They nurtured holiness and loving worship, and were aided by lay-brothers who supported the monastery with their agricultural work.

LIGHT IN DARK AGES

*Missionaries, saints and heroes, the unsung illuminators
of manuscripts, the members of communities,
kings and vassals . . . all make up the rich tapestry of
Christian life lived out in dark times.*

The fall of the Roman Empire certainly did not
mean the extinction of Christianity. As the
barbarians invaded and occupied, Christianity
fought back, winning new lands and peoples.

From north and east came the wandering
tribes, lured on by the fabled riches of Rome.
From Britain came Picts and Scots; from the
Black Sea came Goths; from the north Danes,
Vandals, Angles, Lombards, Jutes and
Burgundians; from the east Teutons and Huns.
All carried with them their own beliefs —
animism or polytheism.

Conversion

Not only did Christianity survive — it began to
hit back. Gregory the Great set out to convert
the newcomers. Born of an aristocratic family,
Gregory turned his back on luxury. He will
always be remembered for his christianization of
southern England. The historian Bede tells how
Gregory saw Saxons for sale in a slave-market,
and declared they should be 'Not Angles, but
angels'.

Gregory dispatched Augustine with forty
monks to England; they won over the king of
Kent and then his people. Thus Augustine
established the centre of Anglican Christianity,
with its cathedral at Canterbury.

The Celts

But Britain was in fact far from pagan. Like
other parts of the empire, England had been
partially converted under the Romans, though
the barbarian invaders eradicated most Christian
traces.

Meanwhile, in Ireland, Patrick had been
cultivating a distinctively Celtic Christianity,
based on severely ascetic monasteries. Their life
centred on prayer, fasting, reading and work.

Following Patrick's conversion of Ireland,
Columba was dispatched to evangelize Scotland,
which he worked on from his base on Iona.
Celtic Christianity, with its saintly heroes and
painstaking manuscript-illuminators, was carried
to Northumbria by Aidan.

With Roman Christianity invading from the
south and Celtic from the north, some
understanding was necessary. A compromise at
the Synod of Whitby (664) ratified a Roman type
of church organization.

Aidan was one of the
missionaries of the ancient
Celtic church, which
developed its own life and
spirituality. The ruins
shown here are the remains
of the monastery he
founded on the
Northumbrian island of
Lindisfarne, off the
north-east coast of
England.

Europe evangelized

It was pioneers from Britain, Willibrord and
Boniface (680-754) — 'apostle to the Germans',
who carried the faith to the north of modern
Germany. Willibrord, at one time a priest in
Ireland, set up a monastery at Echternach from
which further evangelization proceeded. Boniface
set out with a commission from the pope to
convert anybody anywhere. He set about it with
a firm will and a dramatic flair: he is renowned
for boldly chopping down an oak tree sacred to
the god Woden. From its wood he built a new
Christian chapel.

Further north it was Ansgar (–865), the
'apostle of the north', who consolidated the
christianization of Denmark, and who went on to
build the first Christian church in Sweden — a
short-lived success. It took the 'official'
conversion of Denmark by King Cnut to make a

TEACHING AND HEALING

Oxford was among the first universities to be founded in Europe: this was the Divinity School.

From early days, Christianity has fostered and encouraged learning. It is a faith based in a book, the Bible, and in history.

The Emperor Charlemagne was renowned as a patron of education. Alcuin, who took up the torch from the British historian the Venerable Bede, served at Charlemagne's court from 781–96. He explained:

'I . . . endeavour to minister to some the honey of the Scriptures, to intoxicate others with the pure wine of ancient wisdom; others I begin to nourish with the fruits of grammar, and to enlighten many by the order of the stars. But above all things I strive to train them to be useful to the Holy Church of God and for the glory of your kingdom.'

The cathedral schools were centres of learning in eleventh-century Europe. Literacy and theology were encouraged there.

Gatherings of teachers and students — 'universities' — sprang up at Salerno, Bologna and in the school of Notre Dame in Paris. Oxford, Cambridge and other centres soon followed. All were united in their zeal for God, their thirst for knowledge, and their veneration for tradition.

Making men whole
For Jesus, teaching and healing went hand in hand in demonstrating the meaning and power of the 'new age'. The apostles followed his example of both speaking the gospel and bringing wholeness to the body.

From early times, the monks provided medical treatment for the sick as well as aid for the poor. Basil the Great set an example of this in his monastery in Cappadocia in the fourth century. Later, the Franciscans too became noted for their care of the sick — particularly those suffering from leprosy — and encouraged the study of medicine.

Medical missionaries formed a significant proportion in the flood of personnel from Europe and North America in the surge of nineteenth-century missionary enthusiasm, and made great strides in eradicating such diseases as leprosy. In the twentieth century, medically-qualified personnel have remained welcome in many countries where traditional missionaries are now excluded.

lasting impact. Similarly, Norway turned officially Christian under kings Olaf Tryggvissen (–1000) and Olaf Haraldsson (–1050), who were well aware of the political benefits of their decision. In turn, Sweden, Iceland, Greenland and the northern islands were christianized by their Scandinavian invaders.

Eastern expansion

As Europe gradually extended east, the faith was carried to these new territories. King Stephen imposed Christianity upon his subject Magyars; King Wenceslas (929) brought the faith to Bohemia. Polish Christianity flourished under Bloeslaw Chrobry (1025). Repeatedly, the story is of a monarch's conversion being followed, with greater or lesser resistance, by the official christianization of his people.

CRUSADERS AND PILGRIMS

'From the confines of Jerusalem and from the city of Constantinople a horrible tale has gone forth . . . an accursed race, a race utterly alienated from God . . . has invaded the lands of these Christians and depopulated them by the sword, plundering and fire. O most valiant soldiers . . . start upon the road to the Holy Sepulchre, to tear that land from the wicked race and subject it to yourselves.'

With these bloodthirsty words Pope Urban called on Christians of the West to expel the occupying forces from Jerusalem and the Holy Places.

Islam had expanded rapidly and militantly from its birthplace in Arabia. The war-like Seljuk Turks had conquered Jerusalem in 1071 and now, in 1095, threatened Constantinople, the home of Eastern Christianity.

'God wills it'

Urban's sermon was received enthusiastically. Soon Europe was on fire with this new adventure. The warriors of the West united in the 'crusade'. 'God wills it' was their battle-cry. Their banners proudly displayed the cross.

The attraction of the crusade was, first, a military expedition with the pope's blessing and, second, a pilgrimage to the Holy Land. The pope offered various spiritual incentives — especially, an indulgence guaranteeing crusaders access to heaven.

The **First Crusade** gave the whole movement a bad start. A rabble of 50,000 ill-disciplined soldiers descended on Constantinople en route, and disgraced themselves there. But eventually they reached the Holy Land and captured Jerusalem from the Turks in 1099. They attacked at an opportune moment; Islam was temporarily split apart by religious feuding. The victorious crusaders not only occupied Jerusalem but proceeded to set up four crusader states.

Encouraged and enlisted by the pope's representatives throughout Europe, the crusaders set out overland to reclaim Jerusalem from the Turks, finally conquering the city in 1099.

Disgrace

The crusades which followed went from bad to worse. The **Second Crusade** (1147), preached by the saintly Bernard of Clairvaux, ended in military disaster and disgrace. The **Third Crusade**, in which Richard the Lionheart took part, was more successful. But by the **Fourth Crusade** the lust for plunder had supplanted all other motives. Many squalid military expeditions followed — and a regular traffic of warriors, pilgrims and traders plied between Europe and the Holy Land.

Christianity on the march?

Today the crusades fascinate the romantic imagination. But they failed in their aim. A tiny minority of crusaders maintained a toe-hold in the Holy Land — but rather than convert the local people, they tended to take up Eastern customs themselves.

But the crusades did mark a vital turn of a tide. For centuries, Christian Europe had been battered and besieged by pagan forces. Now at last Christianity was on the offensive again — all too literally.

PILGRIMS AND PILGRIMAGES

As early as the fourth century, faithful Christians began to make special visits to holy places — especially sites connected with events in Jesus' life.

Jerusalem took pride of place. Later, Rome became the goal for many pilgrims who wanted to visit the shrines of Peter and Paul, and to see the innumerable relics of saints and martyrs which had been hoarded there.

By the Middle Ages, pilgrimages were almost as popular as holidaying today. The pilgrims wanted to venerate the remains of a saint; they believed that spiritual and physical healing could result from such penitent devotion. But they were also allured by the sights and sounds of foreign travel.

No self-respecting medieval town could hold up its head without a saint's 'relic' in its church. Each new church building had to boast its treasure — whether a bone of Mary Magdalene, a tear of Jesus or a single spike from his crown of thorns. Cities often plundered the treasured relics from a rival centre of attraction.

Favourite shrines for the pilgrims included Rome itself, Canterbury, where the martyred Thomas Becket was honoured, and Santiago de Compostela in northern Spain. To these places the pilgrims journeyed in holiday spirit, travelling in sociable groups, visiting minor shrines on their way. The convivial atmosphere is conveyed in Chaucer's *The Canterbury Tales*, the stories told by a fictitious band of pilgrims to while away their journey.

FRANCIS: THE WAY OF POVERTY

They begged from the rich, gave to the poor, tended the sick and preached to whoever they met.

The flamboyant extravagance of the medieval church scandalized many. Money was poured into church building, and to secure priceless treasures. But many of those who objected to the church's pomp were outlawed as heretics. But one man was different.

Born into the family of an Assisi cloth-merchant in 1182, Francis enjoyed all the luxuries his father could afford. But suddenly, in his twenties, he rejected all this, in literal obedience to Christ's words in the Gospels.

Francis left home clad in the roughest of clothes to take up a wandering life, followed by a few like-minded friends. They begged from the rich, gave to the poor, tended the sick and preached to whoever they met. They often stopped to help restore decaying chapels or shrines.

In time Francis' followers became recognized as a new order: the Franciscans. Francis' friend, Clare, established a similar order for women, the Poor Clares.

It is in giving that we receive

But Francis' insistence on poverty was made in a spirit of adventure, open to the joy of God's created world:

'Praise to Thee, my Lord, for our sister, Mother Earth
Who sustains and directs us
And brings forth varied fruits and coloured flowers and plants.'

Many people link Francis with the birds and animals, who, legend claims, listened spellbound to his sermons. In fact, most of his efforts were devoted to the mushrooming cities of medieval Italy, where he preached and cared for the impoverished.

Francis had a magnetic personality; but he realized that his followers would be tempted with riches and power after his death. His last command was:

'Let all the brothers beware of accepting churches, houses or anything else provided for them unless they conform to holy poverty.'

Yet soon after his death in 1226 a massive basilica to his memory was erected in Assisi itself.

Missionaries

Missions were a key concern of the Franciscans. Francis himself managed to get to Egypt in 1219, where, dirty and penniless, he surrendered to the Muslim guards, demanding an audience with the Sultan. The Muslim leader heard him preach — but turned down Francis' offer to firewalk to prove his faith.

The Franciscans went on to send brothers to Hungary, Spain and the East, and established houses in Eastern Europe, North Africa and the Middle East in the thirteenth century. Later, missionaries travelled as far as Central Asia and India, and an Archbishop of the East was appointed near Peking in the fourteenth century.

The Franciscans continued to lead the way as missionaries. The Spanish and Portuguese conquest of the New World was rapidly followed

up by the friars — with Franciscans to the fore. They immediately set about converting the native population, and often attempted to adapt Christianity for the new adherents.

Young people in Zimbabwe attend a baptismal class run by a Franciscan mission. Ever since Francis of Assisi's day, Franciscans have been active in social, pastoral, educational and missionary work.

THE FRIARS

Francis' followers, the Franciscans, were often nicknamed 'Grey Friars' from their grey habit; it distinguished them from the 'Black Friars' — or Dominicans. The friars were a new force in the church; preaching-monks, who spent much of their time in the towns and cities, gaining popular respect by their simple living and their caring.

The Dominicans, founded by Dominic de Guzman (1170–1221) pursued learning, and were closely involved in the rise of the new universities — Paris, Bologna and later Oxford and Cambridge. But the Franciscans had their intellectuals too: Bonaventura, Duns Scotus, William of Ockham and Roger Bacon.

Lord, make me an instrument of thy peace.
Where there is hatred, let me sow love;
Where there is injury, pardon;
Where there is doubt, faith;
Where there is despair, hope;
Where there is darkness, light;
Where there is sadness, joy.

O Divine Master, grant that
I may not so much seek to be consoled, as to console;
Not so much to be understood as to understand;
Not so much to be loved as to love;
For it is in giving that we receive;
It is in pardoning that we are pardoned;
It is in dying that we awaken to eternal life.

Attributed to Francis of Assisi

THE CATHEDRAL BUILDERS

Religious fervour was the driving force behind the great period of cathedral building during the Middle Ages. But civic pride and rivalry also played their part.

Perhaps the most familiar — and fitting — image of the medieval church is the cathedral. These massive structures sprang up all over Western Europe, particularly France and England, vying with one another in size and magnificence. Old St Paul's, London, totalled 585 feet in length; Winchester Cathedral only slightly less at 526 feet. The cathedrals of France leapt ever higher: Notre Dame, Paris, was 110 feet high; Chartres, 114 feet; Rheims, 125 feet; and Beauvais, 154. Nearly 200 cathedrals were built in the Gothic style in the thirteenth and fourteenth centuries.

Faith and vision

The cathedrals tell much about medieval Christianity. They were invariably built in the loftiest part of the city, and dominate the houses clustered below. The cathedral was an undertaking of faith, breathtaking in its vision, serene in its confidence. But it also reflects the vast riches of the church, contrasting with the poverty of the masses who contributed to its construction.

The structure of the Gothic cathedral is light and soaring. Support was provided outside by 'flying buttresses'; the pointed arches gave a sense of reaching towards heaven. Inside some there was mystery, in others brilliance and lightness. Stained-glass windows glowed with 'sermons in colour'. Every inch of stonework and glass was sculpted, or carved, or painted, or adorned.

The master craftsmen

Some writers have suggested that pious citizens joined in voluntary labour to build the cathedrals. But in fact building operations were tightly organized, carefully financed, and professionally managed. Neither the priests nor the people helped in the construction work. Masons travelled from one site to the next, jealously protecting their craft — the origin of the 'lodges' of 'freemasons' today.

Normally the bishop or chapter found a master-mason to undertake the job; he was designer, builder and manager rolled into one. Some of the great English master-masons included Master Robert (St Albans), William of Sens (Canterbury) and William of Colchester (York).

Craftsmen were recruited from the various specialist guilds and paid at the going rate. To finance the work, the bishop had to raise vast amounts of cash — by selling spiritual privileges, by begging-missions, and by employing fund-raisers. It was the scandal of the professional money-raisers, selling indulgences on behalf of the rebuilding of St Peter's at Rome, that was later to provoke Martin Luther to action. But a cathedral housing a popular shrine, such as that of Thomas Becket at Canterbury, could earn valuable cash from the entrance-fees of the visiting hordes of pilgrims.

The floodlit nave and apse of Chartres Cathedral, France, convey the soaring magnificence of the Gothic cathedral — one of the peaks of medieval artistic achievement.

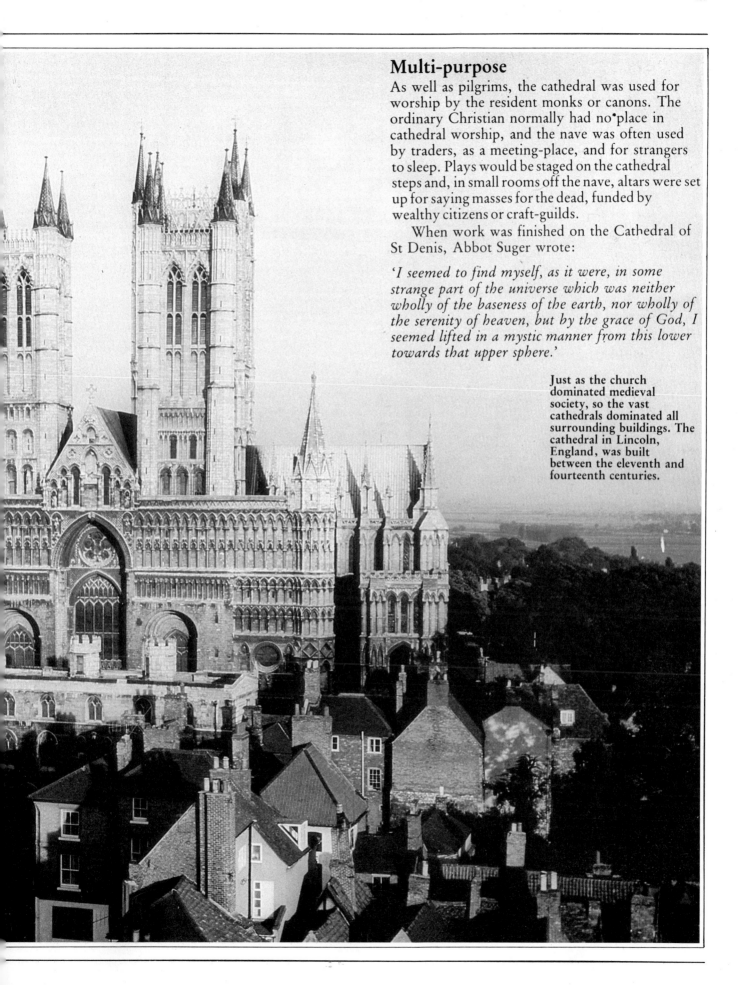

Multi-purpose

As well as pilgrims, the cathedral was used for worship by the resident monks or canons. The ordinary Christian normally had no place in cathedral worship, and the nave was often used by traders, as a meeting-place, and for strangers to sleep. Plays would be staged on the cathedral steps and, in small rooms off the nave, altars were set up for saying masses for the dead, funded by wealthy citizens or craft-guilds.

When work was finished on the Cathedral of St Denis, Abbot Suger wrote:

'I seemed to find myself, as it were, in some strange part of the universe which was neither wholly of the baseness of the earth, nor wholly of the serenity of heaven, but by the grace of God, I seemed lifted in a mystic manner from this lower towards that upper sphere.'

Just as the church dominated medieval society, so the vast cathedrals dominated all surrounding buildings. The cathedral in Lincoln, England, was built between the eleventh and fourteenth centuries.

THE PEAKS OF LEARNING

'Believe in order to understand.'
Augustine

Just as the twelfth century saw the soaring cathedrals, so there appeared a succession of towering theologians to systematize and categorize Christian ideas. They set out to present theology in terms that were agreeable with contemporary philosophy.

The scholastics

Anselm, Archbishop of Canterbury in the late eleventh century, is famous for his logical argument for the existence of God. He also wrote on Christ's death on the cross — *Cur Deus Homo* — *Why did God become man?* He answered that only God-Man (Christ) could make a satisfactory compensation for human sin.

A second master-mind, **Peter Abelard**, attacked some of Anselm's ideas. His illicit love-affair with his pupil Héloise has scandalized and fascinated, but he was equally daring in his thinking. He repeatedly touched on the root of problems, and attracted the suspicions of less searching scholars. His views on the Trinity and on Christ's death on the cross were too radical for safety.

Thomas Aquinas was a giant in body and mind. He attracted the nickname of 'dumb-ox' since he was fat, slow and serious. Yet these features screened a brilliant mind and a prolific pen. Among a shelf-ful of works he wrote the hugely influential *Summa Theologica* and *Summa Contra Gentiles*, a kind of encyclopaedia of Christian thought. He reigned supreme in the medieval thinkers' task of bringing together rational and revealed truth. But when reason and the faith of the apostles appeared to clash, the weight of the church's authority was enough to make Aquinas plump for revealed truth.

Education was very much a concern of the church. The thinking of the intellectual giants — all monks and clergy — was carried on against the background of classical Greek philosophy, the Bible and the teaching of the early Christian writers.

God be in my head,
And in my understanding;

God be in my eyes,
And in my looking;

God be in my mouth,
And in my speaking;

God be in my heart,
And in my thinking;

God be at my end,
And at my departing.

Sarum Missal

AUGUSTINE

Like Janus, the Roman god of the New Year, Augustine stands at the turning-point. He lived at the close of the initial period of the church's growth, when the Roman Empire was crumbling into decay. But he also looks ahead to the church of the Middle Ages, which he strongly influenced.

Although he was brought up in Roman North Africa by his believing mother, Monnica, it was as an adult that his life was revolutionized. While reading from his Bible, 'it was as though the light of faith flooded into my heart and all the darkness of doubt was dispelled'.

He plunged into a life of preaching and teaching, and became a redoubtable defender of orthodox Christianity. One key to the Christian faith was: 'Believe in order to understand.' His books, the *Confessions* and the *City of God*, have profoundly affected generations of Christians. Living through the turmoil of a collapsing empire, he encouraged believers to seek the peace of the kingdom of heaven.

Manuscripts were laboriously copied by hand to make additional copies available. These handwritten texts were often illuminated: ornamental designs, letters and paintings decorated manuscripts of all kinds, particularly religious ones.

WINDS OF CHANGE

'We ask God then of his supreme goodness to reform our church, as being entirely out of joint, to the perfectness of its first beginning.'
The Lollard Conclusions, 1394

The medieval church was remarkable not only for its gigantic achievements — but also for its abuses. Devotional practices declined into magical rites. Priests were corrupt, and often ignorant. Religious leaders were concerned more for grandeur and pompous buildings than humble service.

But throughout the centuries men and women appeared to counter this decay. Some challenged quietly, reforming their own lives. Others experimented, trying to find a life-style closer to Christ's way and forming church groups on a New Testament pattern. Still others sounded a prophetic note, calling society to reform.

The simple life
In about 1175, for instance, Peter Waldo experienced conversion to Christ, took up a simple life of poverty and preaching, and had translations made of the New Testament into the local language as a basis of his evangelism. The 'Waldensians', or 'Poor Men of Lyons', spread throughout Europe, linking up with other like-minded groups.

In the Low Countries, a new form of Christian community was founded in the fourteenth century. Named the Brotherhood of the Common Life, it was less tightly disciplined than earlier monastic orders, and encouraged both devotion and learning. The brothers hammered out new ideas, copied manuscripts, and worshipped together. Thomas à Kempis, probably the author of the famous *Imitation of Christ*, was attracted to join one of these communities at Windesheim. The emotional depth of his book is typical of the sensitive Christ-centred nature of the Brotherhood.

Thomas à Kempis was a spiritual leader of the late medieval church.

John Wyclif was a scholar who rediscovered in the New Testament a gospel of new life in Christ. He did much to make the Bible known, and translated the Latin *Vulgate* Bible into English.

Thomas à Kempis

John Wyclif

The followers of Jan Hus in Bohemia — the Hussites — renamed their towns with Bible place-names. Here in Tábor, they re-established the Bible's practice of sharing both the bread and wine of the communion.

Jan Hus

Girolamo Savonarola

Discovery

But there were other more daring opponents of corruption and deadness. In Spain, Cardinal Ximenes (–1517) rejected all pomp and privilege, and set an example of holy living. He encouraged the study of the ancient languages of the Bible and the reform of the clergy and monastic orders. However he also encouraged the forced conversion by the Inquisition of non-Christians in Spanish lands.

The rediscovery of the Bible and renewed interest in ancient languages brought by the Renaissance encouraged scholars to read it afresh. The Czech reformer Jan Hus found there a gospel of freedom and new life in Christ. His movement spread quickly to people who were impatient with the bondage of the Holy Roman Empire. The communion cup, given now to all, not just the priests, became their symbol. Hus was vainly supported by Czech nationalists, but was condemned for heresy and burned in 1415.

In England John Wyclif, discovering the message and authority of the Scriptures, attacked the moral and theological shortcomings of Rome. He escaped the fate of a condemned heretic since he had influential friends. He gave rise to itinerant groups of 'Lollard' preachers, whose beliefs spread across England and further.

Challenge

Most colourful of all was the Italian reformer Girolamo Savonarola (–1498). A dedicated ascetic, he denounced the paganism of Renaissance Florence, gaining a massive popular following, and becoming first citizen. But when summoned to Rome to explain himself, he began to attack the pope and the church, and was eventually excommunicated, hanged and burned.

The Renaissance, with its new emphasis on man as an independent being, also cut away at the authority of Rome. Much of the new learning stemmed from classical Greece and Rome, and was pagan in its tendency. The church no longer reigned supreme as sole source of learning.

Jan Hus became a martyr in the cause of church reform and Czech nationalism.

Girolamo Savonarola was an Italian preacher whose opposition to the papacy eventually brought about his execution.

MARTIN LUTHER

'The righteous shall live by faith.' By faith?
Not by the painful works of mortifying the flesh, but
by simple trust in Christ? How could this be?

The sale of 'indulgences' had grown into a scandal. By paying money towards the rebuilding of St Peter's Basilica in Rome, the people were promised a shorter time in purgatory. Luther saw the trade in indulgences as turning people away from God's forgiveness freely available through Christ.

Martin Luther was born into a miner's family in Germany, and educated at Erfurt University. There amidst a violent thunderstorm, he took the sudden decision in 1505 to become a monk, against his father's wishes. Full of doubts, he found that neither the round of confession and penance, nor a trip to Rome as a pilgrim and sightseer satisfied him.

The unquiet monk turned to the study of the Bible — and on a crucial occasion came face to face with the living God. He grasped the apostle Paul's words in his letter to the Romans, 'The righteous shall live by faith'. By faith? Not by the painful works of mortifying the flesh, but by simple trust in Christ? How could this be?

In October 1517 there came to Wittenberg Johannes Tetzel, selling indulgences, which he promised would keep his customers out of purgatory. Luther was stung to action: on the university notice-board (the church door) he posted his '95 Theses' for debate, focussing on the abuse of indulgences.

'Here I stand'

Luther's rediscovery of a message of repentance and faith undermined the whole confessional system of the medieval church — indulgences, pilgrimages, penances and the rest. He was called to defend his views, but had gained allies among priests, scholars, humanists and the German people.

Luther now began to speak of the pope as Anti-Christ, since he was obstructing the free course of the gospel; monasteries, the mass and penance all perverted God's grace. From reading the New Testament Luther realized that if salvation depended on man, it was worthless and hopeless. Faith — God's gift in Christ — was the only hope for salvation.

At the Diet of Worms in 1521 Luther turned down his last opportunity to retreat; he would not — he could not — recant. He stood by the authority of the Bible.

Fortunately he had powerful friends, and was hidden at the Wartburg Castle, where he set himself the crucial and formative task of translating the Bible into German.

The result was to bring the Bible to the people in a new way. The new technology of printing was harnessed to bring it to a mass audience. At the same time pamphlets and counter-pamphlets, books, even hymns set to popular tunes, carried the message to the hearts and lives of the people.

The new movement

Meanwhile in Switzerland, Ulrich Zwingli (–1531), a milder but more radical reformer, was at work. For him, the riches of Renaissance learning were vital to the faith. He became embroiled in politics, dying on the battlefield, and was not afraid to defy the traditions of the

Following his refusal to renounce his 'heresies', Luther the outlaw found refuge at Wartburg Castle under the protection of Frederick of Saxony. Here he translated the Bible into German — a crucial event not only for the development of the German language, but for the whole future of the Reformation.

'I cannot and I will not recant anything, for to go against conscience is neither right nor safe. Here I stand. I cannot do otherwise. God help me. Amen.'
Martin Luther, 18 April 1521

Luther's views became public when he pinned his '95 Theses' to the university notice-board, the church door at Wittenberg. Statues of Melanchthon and Luther now stand in the town square.

church. Born in Wildhaus, he began to reform when he was made minister at Zürich. He too taught that it was solely by God's initiative that salvation came to a person.

Zwingli's views were overtaken by those of Calvin and of the Anabaptists. By contrast, Luther's ideas spread widely. Soon many of the German principalities and little states were committed to Lutheranism. Philip Melanchthon systematized Luther's thought; artists such as Dürer, Cranach and Holbein joined the reform movement. But Luther's midway position alienated some people — for example, those who wanted to reject completely the church's ceremonies, or her reliance on secular rulers. But Luther trusted in the preaching of the Word to continue the work of reformation. The last thing he wanted was for his message to be hardened into a new scholasticism to replace the old . . .

Gradually new religious boundaries were drawn, sometimes decided by military force. At the Peace of Augsburg (1555), final divisions were recognized; each state was to take the religion of its ruler. It was to form the pattern of Catholic/Protestant areas that can still be seen in Germany and middle-Europe today.

JOHN CALVIN

A quiet and sensitive man in contrast to the aggressively forthright Luther, John Calvin nonetheless had a profound influence on the progress of the Reformation.

John Calvin was twenty-five years younger than Luther and grew up in a world where Protestantism was becoming established. A Frenchman, he was born in Noyon, Picardy, in 1509, and given a full humanist education at the University of Paris. Even as a student, his personal severity and devotion to learning were obvious — and probably began to erode his health.

Ideas

In his early twenties, Calvin was converted to Christian faith and devoted more and more of his energies to theology. His genius for systematizing ideas was becoming evident. In 1536 he published his biblical theology, *The Institution of the Christian Religion*. From this point his basic ideas never altered; they were simply elaborated or clarified.

In many ways, Calvin echoed Luther. Man is sinful: he cannot possibly fulfil God's requirements, left to his own resources. He can be righteous, accepted in God's sight, only through faith in Christ, for Christ died for our sins.

But then for us to know God is what we were created for: 'Man's chief end is to glorify God and to enjoy him for ever.' God is known through what we can see of him as Creator, through his self-revelation in the Bible, and as Saviour of the world in Christ.

Many have reacted against Calvin's rigorous logic when it came to the idea of 'predestination':

'Always I have faithfully attempted what I believed to be for the glory of God.'
John Calvin

'God has mercy on whom he has mercy; and whom he will he hardens.' But, for Calvin, the Bible was the supreme authority, and he aimed to present systematically what he saw to be its teachings.

Action

Calvin — a Frenchman — cannot be separated from Geneva in Switzerland. Yet it was against his will that he ever settled there. In 1536, while passing through the city, Calvin was virtually terrorized into staying by the reformer William Farel.

Calvin responded by trying to make Geneva a model City of God among men, identifying town and church as one and the same. By controlling the church and education, Calvin tried to control the morals, commerce, ideas and policies of the city. Naturally the free-minded citizens objected. The logic of his position even led Calvin to the notorious act of executing the foolhardy Michael Servetus for denying the Trinity. Calvin and Farel were ousted in 1538, but Calvin was recalled and managed to remain in the city until his death.

After Calvin's death, Geneva became a haven for fugitive Protestants, training and equipping them to return home, taking with them the teachings of Calvinism, notably to France, Holland and Scotland.

Calvin wanted to bring every citizen of Geneva under the moral discipline of the church.

WILLIAM TYNDALE AND THE ENGLISH BIBLE

Most of the translation of the 'Authorized' or King James Version of the Bible was his: yet he had to flee for his life . . .

As a young man, William Tyndale promised a priest:

'If God spares my life, ere many years pass, I will cause a boy that drives the plough to know more of the Scriptures than thou dost.'

Educated at Magdalen Hall, Oxford, and probably at Cambridge University too, William Tyndale became appalled by the ignorance of parish priests while he was tutoring for a Gloucestershire family. It was this that helped persuade him to try to translate the Bible into English.

Since 1480, the English Bible had been banned, partly because the *Wyclif Bible* had been used by the outlawed Lollards. Tyndale wanted to make a better translation: rather than translating from the Latin *Vulgate* (as the *Wyclif Bible* had done) he would work from the original Greek and Hebrew of the New and Old Testaments, using the new learning of Renaissance Europe.

Life at risk

Optimistically, Tyndale hoped to win the English bishops' support for his task; but they feared it would help spread Lutheran ideas. When it became clear that he could not safely remain in England, Tyndale fled to Europe to complete his translation. Even then his life was at risk; he completed work on the New Testament, but had to leave Cologne before it could be published.

The first complete book known to have been printed in the Christian world was the Bible, in 1456. Printing was established throughout Europe by the end of the fifteenth century. It met a great new demand for reading material and made possible the rapid spread of the Reformation.

'In the beginning God created the heaven and the earth. And the earth was without form, and void; and darkness was upon the face of the deep. And the Spirit of God moved upon the face of the waters.

And God said, Let there be light: and there was light.'

Genesis 1:1 in the words of the King James, or Authorized, Version of the Bible

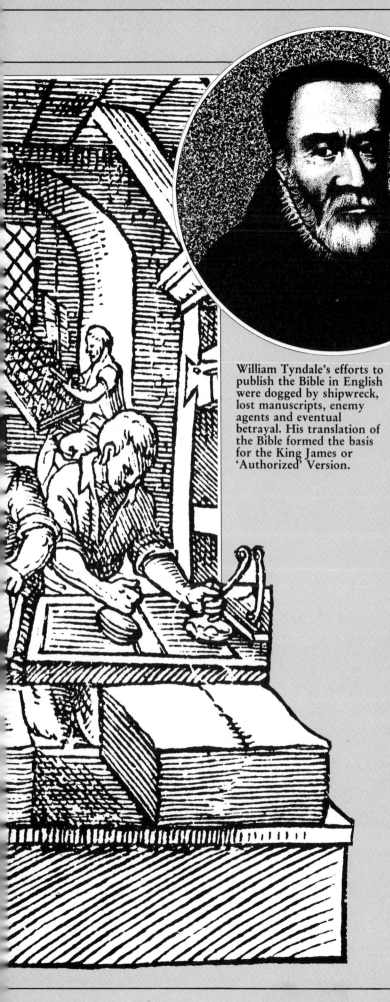

William Tyndale's efforts to publish the Bible in English were dogged by shipwreck, lost manuscripts, enemy agents and eventual betrayal. His translation of the Bible formed the basis for the King James or 'Authorized' Version.

Tyndale now proceeded to the Old Testament, finishing work on several of its books. But his task was interrupted by enemies who had him arrested near Brussels in 1535. The following year he was burnt at the stake, his task still unfinished.

Tyndale's work was completed by Miles Coverdale, whose Bible was published in 1535, followed by the *Matthew Bible* in 1537, revised by Coverdale to become the *Great Bible* (1539).

Authorized Version

The *King James Version* did not appear until the beginning of the seventeenth century; it resulted from Puritans lobbying King James I of England. Published in 1611, it is often known as the *Authorized Version*, and retains much from previous translations. But it soon became the dominant version in English, coinciding with a 'golden' period in English literary style.

However, it is no exaggeration to say that every English New Testament before the twentieth century is a revision of Tyndale's. Roughly ninety per cent of the words of his New Testament were used in the *King James Version*, and about seventy-five per cent in the *Revised Standard Version*.

'Blessed Lord, who has caused all holy Scriptures to be written for our learning; Grant that we may in such wise hear them, read, mark, learn, and inwardly digest them, that by patience, and comfort of thy holy Word, we may embrace, and ever hold fast the blessed hope of everlasting life.'

The Book of Common Prayer, 1662

EUROPE REFORMED

Luther may have provided the Reformation movement with its chief source of energy and vision. But there were Christians throughout Europe ready and waiting to take up the cause.

Britain's break with Rome was possible only because England had a history of reforming movements, a cluster of humanist scholars, and regular traffic with continental Lutherans. The apparent reason was Henry VIII's desire for a male heir — and boredom with his queen, Catherine of Aragon. But the real reasons were again the rediscovery of the Bible and the gospel.

Henry passed the necessary Acts of Parliament to break with Rome, but was not enthusiastic about any shift in beliefs. He became the 'only supreme head on earth of the Church of England'. He also took the drastic step of dissolving all the monasteries.

Henry's archbishop was the apparently mild Thomas Cranmer, who encouraged the use of the English Bible in the churches, and shaped the masterly English prose-style of *The Book of Common Prayer*. (He was later burnt at the stake by Mary Tudor in her vain effort to restore the pope's supremacy.)

It was under Elizabeth I that Anglicanism was finally established, the Queen herself defining the 'middle way', which rejected the more extreme Protestantism of the Presbyterians.

The Scots

Meanwhile to the north, John Knox brought thorough Calvinism to Scotland. Still independent, Scotland had been prepared for reform by Lollards, by humanists and by nationalistic feelings.

John Knox returned from exile in Calvin's Geneva to join the Scots' cause against Catholicism and against the French party headed by Mary Queen of Scots. Parliament established Protestantism in 1560, and a Confession of Faith and 'Book of Discipline' followed, based on an uncompromising Calvinism.

Reformation Europe was a divided Europe. Large areas still gave Rome their allegiance, while Lutheran and Calvinist ideas extended their influence mainly to northern Europe.

Spread of the new faith

After Luther's death in 1546, his cause spread rapidly into Scandinavia. King Christian II (–1523) had tried to enforce reform in Denmark. But genuine reform only began by the efforts of Paul Eliae, a Lutheran humanist in Copenhagen. Frederick I finished the task of creating an 'official' Lutheran reformation in Denmark. In Sweden it was Gustavus Vasa (–1560), maker of the modern state, who established Lutheranism, aided by the theologians Lars and Olavus Petri from Wittenberg. A Swedish New Testament was published, and Iceland and Norway soon followed Sweden. Finland was guided into the Lutheran fold by King Michael Agricola (1508–57).

Lutheranism also spread to the east. Poland was divided; the Unitarian ideas of Sozzini were equally popular. Hungary, with its strong Germanic influences, was attracted to Lutheranism; Czechoslovakia had its own Hussite reform, but was also influenced by Lutheran ideas.

Faith and nationalism

Calvinist or Reformed Protestantism flourished elsewhere. From Geneva and Strasbourg it spread to some of the south German states, and to parts of Poland and east Germany. Calvinism spread in France, despite persecution. Reformed ideas also flourished in the Low Countries, through which Calvinist refugees from Britain and France passed.

For some it was a message of liberation and hope. For others, it was a territorial 'change of religion', used by nationalist forces to try to win independence. Calvin's Geneva as a Christian city-state was not always a helpful model, particularly when man fought his neighbour in the cause of religion. In France the problem of co-existence was solved only by the ejection of the Protestants, the Huguenots — and so a sizeable proportion of the French middle classes — a hundred years later.

PIETY AND OUTREACH

'Teach us, good Lord, to serve thee as thou deservest; to give and not to count the cost; to fight and not to heed the wounds; to toil and not to ask for rest; to labour and not to ask for any reward save knowing that we do thy will.'

Ignatius Loyola was another great religious pioneer of the sixteenth century. Born in 1491 at the castle of Loyola, in the Basque region of northern Spain, he grew up a rich gallant. But his prospects of a military career were shattered by a cannon-ball which crippled him during a siege. In a period of self-questioning, Ignatius began to read the Bible and lives of the saints, resolving to become a soldier of Christ, a kind of romantic, self-denying saint: 'St Dominic did this, therefore I have to do it. St Francis did this, therefore I have to do it.'

Consecration

Ignatius now wrote the *Spiritual Exercises*, a detailed and demanding set of devotions for breaking in new recruits for Jesus. The four-week crash-course, emphasizing the horrors of hell, the Gospel stories, the example of Christ, and absolute obedience to Rome, soon became popular.

'Always be ready to obey with mind and heart, setting aside all judgment of one's own, the true spouse of Jesus Christ, our holy mother, our infallible orthodox mistress, the Catholic Church, whose authority is exercised over us by the hierarchy.'

The thirty-three-year-old Loyola, his energies newly-channelled, pursued his studies at the universities of Alcala, Salamanca and Paris. He attracted disciples, and formed the Society of Jesus in 1534, whose members vowed to dedicate their lives to Christ. Because of his puritanical extremism — Loyola lived as a hermit for a time, growing his hair and nails long — he came under suspicion by the Inquisition. However, he gained recognition by boldly offering the society's obedience to Pope Paul III.

The Jesuits

The Order was designed for the modern world; its rankings were like those of a modern army.

The members wore no uniform, and women were barred. The Jesuits devoted themselves to education, reform, spiritual discipline and missions. They introduced rigorous educational methods, providing schooling for all ages from primary to university, and specialized in educating the upper classes. In this way they buttressed the faith of the ruling classes of Europe.

Jesuit schools emphasized how the Catholic faith fitted into the existing social order based on privilege, hierarchy and ceremonial. They

South America has been the scene of much missionary activity. In the sixteenth and seventeenth centuries, Jesuit missionaries worked extensively in the continent. Protestant churches today, such as this Baptist congregation in Bolivia, are flourishing and expanding.

sailed to Goa, off the Indian coast. Although sea-sick, he baptized thousands before travelling on to Sri Lanka, Malaysia and Japan, dying while waiting to enter China.

Xavier has been criticized for adapting the faith, for using the Inquisition, and for approving persecution — but his example fired thousands to follow. Dominicans and others went with merchants and explorers to India, the Americas and Asia, baptizing the masses into an often dimly-understood faith. Jesuit strategy was to aim to win the ruler's allegiance to Christ, so that he would in turn legislate the conversion of his people.

The Jesuits met no success in China, although they lived in Peking for two centuries, and their astronomy and mathematics were admired. In Japan, many were converted by the end of the sixteenth century, but vicious persecution totally eradicated Christianity in the following decades.

SOUTH AMERICA

In 1492 Columbus discovered America, as every schoolboy knows. Portugal and Spain vied for the New World; Pope Alexander VI drew a line down the Atlantic, declaring that all land to the west of it belonged to Spain, all land to the east to Portugal. Forward went the adventurers, the merchants and the priests to make new conquests.

Cortes came to Mexico and found the advanced Aztec civilization. Following the armies came the priests, baptizing the uncomprehending Indians in their masses, but making little attempt to instruct them in Christian beliefs. Often they were treated as little more than slaves by their Spanish masters.

The result of this rapid and superficial conversion was that many pagan customs and beliefs were swept up into Mexican Christianity. Often early Christian crosses from Mexico have Aztec sacred objects concealed inside them. The two religions were merged to make a single, muddled system.

This mingling of beliefs has continued down to the present in such countries as Guatemala, Peru and Dominique, where primitive practices are still to be seen.

Protestantism has mushroomed in South America in the twentieth century. In 1914 there were less than half a million Protestants in the entire continent, and they were often oppressed. By 1968, Protestants were estimated at more than 10 million, of whom over seventy-five per cent lived in Brazil.

The greatest expansion in South America has been among the Pentecostals, who number more than sixty per cent of all Protestants. The Protestant churches of South America are strong: they have local leaders, and are normally self-supporting.

fostered drama, the Baroque arts and architecture. By these means the Jesuits built bulwarks of the Counter-Reformation against Protestantism in such countries as Austria, Bavaria, Poland and parts of the Rhineland.

Missions

But the Jesuits are known above all for their missions, following in the steps of Francis Xavier (–1552). He met Loyola in Paris, becoming one of the first Jesuits. He was dedicated to convert as much of mankind as possible, and in 1542

ROME RESPONDS

The Protestant Reformation sparked off varied and sometimes far-reaching reactions from a Roman Catholic church seeking to re-assert its authority.

While many reformers ended far beyond the limits of the Roman church, others remained faithful to Rome, contributing to a new spirit of devotion.

For instance, in Rome itself a new community of believers was formed in 1517, the 'Oratory of Divine Love', with members from all sections of society — workmen, scholars and ordinary Christians, united in service and prayer.

Piety

Meanwhile in Spain, among several mystics, there appeared Teresa (–1582), whose spirituality has inspired many. Like St John of the Cross, her meditations on the life of Christ were marked by heights of ecstasy and depths of despair.

Rome also responded to the Reformation by tightening up her organization. A great council met at Trent, in northern Italy, between 1545 and 1563. But it admitted no faults in the past, and simply re-defined and re-emphasized traditional views.

Shock-waves

Rome received more shocks with the growth of national consciousness and the rise of the absolute rulers. For example, in 1682 the French clergy declared that the pope and the church had no authority over the secular rulers. In response to pressures from the rulers of France, Portugal and Spain, the Society of Jesus, with its absolute loyalty to the pope, was abolished in 1773. The Jesuits were only revived in 1814, with the restoration of the old monarchies of Europe, following the Napoleonic Wars.

The reform movement in the Roman Catholic church during the sixteenth and seventeenth centuries, the 'Counter-Reformation', re-emphasized the authority of the church, the mysteries of religion and the drama of the mass. It was given expression in the baroque style of architecture. With their elaborate decoration and dramatic visual effects, the baroque churches gave people a sense of awe and wonder, and overwhelmed them with splendour and magnificence.

Rome reeled with the coming of the French Revolution. The Enlightenment thinking, revolutionary politics and egalitarian atmosphere all undermined traditional Catholicism. Although Napoleon restored the church, he cynically used it for his own ends.

Claims

The church later identified itself with the reactionary regimes of Europe — Metternich in Austria, Louis Napoleon in France — so that in 1830 and 1848 the revolutionaries trained their sights on this symbol of rich irrelevance. Some churchmen tried to save the day by working to separate church and state — but in vain.

One Catholic reaction to these assaults was to make grander and grander claims. With no biblical backing, Pope Pius promulgated the new dogma of the Immaculate Conception in 1854. The Vatican Council of 1870 offended other Christian churches by claiming official infallibility for the pope.

Even some Catholics objected to this new doctrine, but were excommunicated for their pains. The church hit back ineffectively with the Syllabus of Errors (1864), which listed forbidden 'modern' movements — toleration, socialism, Bible Societies, pantheism, rationalism, liberalism among others.

This tendency to compromise with reactionary political movements has damaged the Catholic church in the twentieth century. Pius XI treated with Mussolini, and blessed as a 'Holy War' his Abyssinian campaign. He was more wary with Hitler, but made arrangements with the dictators in Spain, Portugal and Austria, hoping to buttress them against communism, which proved a bitter enemy in Poland, Hungary and Yugoslavia.

New openness

Since the Vatican II Council of 1962–65, however, there has been a fresh approach in many areas. With new liturgies and the mass in local languages, a new emphasis on Bible reading, a willingness to reconsider issues which were previously simply matters of 'authority', plus an openness to new ideas and new methods, Rome is tackling once again the challenge of being 'the church in the world'

DISSENT: ANABAPTISTS AND NONCONFORMISTS

'The Lord has more truth yet to break forth out of his holy Word.'

John Robinson, leader of the 'Pilgrim Fathers', as they set sail for America in 1620

Throughout medieval history there had been dissenting groups returning to a simpler Christian life-style. With the coming of the Bible in their own languages, such radical movements spread all over northern Europe. Some rejected the traditions of the church, or the priesthood, or the sacraments. Some simply gathered for prayer and the study of the Bible, or for mutual fellowship within or outside the recognized churches.

Personal faith

Many of these groups rejected infant baptism, demanding re-baptism; hence their label 'Anabaptist', particularly in Switzerland from the 1520s. The Anabaptists believed that the church consisted only of those who have personal faith. They wanted a New Testament simplicity in their form of worship and organization; for them, communion expressed their fellowship and reminded them of Christ's sacrifice.

The label 'Anabaptist' included a large number of different groups of varying emphasis. Those following the ex-Lutheran Thomas Münzer, for instance, did not hesitate to use

Desperate to escape religious persecution, the Pilgrim Fathers crowded onto the *Mayflower* to cross the Atlantic in 1620 to Plymouth, Massachusetts, where this replica of the ship can now be seen.

Originating among the Anabaptists of central Europe, the Mennonites now have their largest following in North America. Some of them are known for their strict simplicity of worship and a life-style which has little, if anything, in common with the American way of life.

violence. But more typical were the pacifists, such as the Hutterites of Austria, who formed their own communities. Others again had more sectarian teachings, for instance about Christ's second coming.

Menno Simons (1561) presented his beliefs more systematically than most. In time he attracted a following — the Mennonites — distinguished by non-resistance, non-obedience to the state when it went against Scripture, and by an attempt to keep the church pure.

Baptism

In England, the Anabaptists as such did not attract many followers. But there was already a tradition of Lollards and other groups who objected to such things as priests' robes, lavish music for worship and traditional liturgy. Congregationalists began to found churches independent of the state, again formed only of believers, and with each church independent though linked in fellowship. The Baptists went further, saying that baptism was only for adults as an expression of their faith in Christ, not for infants.

The preface still printed in every King James, or Authorized Version, of the Bible referred to 'Popish persons' on the one hand and, on the other, 'self-conceited brethren, who run their own ways, and give liking unto nothing but what is framed by themselves . . . ' Such was the price of freedom.

With the victory of Oliver Cromwell's puritan forces in the English Revolution came a chance to experiment with every shape of Christian grouping, from the violent Fifth Monarchy Men and Fox's Quakers to the free-loving Ranters.

The return of the monarchy, in the shape of King Charles II, brought the re-establishment of the Church of England. For a time dissent was persecuted and oppressed; but it had come to stay, and was first tolerated, then accepted as a British institution. One-time sects became respectable denominations — Presbyterians, Congregationalists, Baptists, the Society of Friends.

To the New World

The puritans also had great influence in the New World. From the beginning of the seventeenth century, bands of persecuted or pioneering pilgrims set out for America, hoping to find religious liberty and a new life. With their militant faith and practical drive, they shaped a thriving, moralistic society, which fuelled the energy of the modern USA. The puritans' trust in the workings of Providence, their iron sense of vocation, and resolve to do their great taskmaster's work all contributed to the ideals of twentieth-century America.

THE MUSIC OF CHRISTIANITY

Part of the rich cultural heritage of Christianity is the variety of music it has inspired — whether haunting plainsong, uplifting oratorio or the modern box-office success.

The psalmist invited us to praise God 'with lute and harp', 'with strings and pipe' and 'with loud clashing cymbals'. Yet the monks of the centuries following the fall of the Roman Empire regarded musical instruments as fit merely for secular music — for minstrels and troubadours. They opted for the human voice alone.

Plainsong

The musical basis of the Roman Catholic church became the Gregorian chant. Named after Pope Gregory, who in about AD 600 standardized the tunes used in worship, it included music for every service and every festival of the church. Gregorian chant — one form of plainsong — has been sung unchanged for over 1,000 years. Many of the tunes are much older; some come from classical Greece and Rome, others from Jewish synagogue worship.

Plainsong has no harmony. Its rhythm is the rhythm of the words chanted. The tunes cover only a narrow span of notes. But heard in a vast cathedral they sound forth magnificently. Plainsong is widely used in the Eastern churches too: in the chants of the Byzantine, Syrian and Armenian churches, for example.

Concerts

Some chants are simple enough to be sung by regular congregations; others are more complex, and best left to the choir. In the past, every cathedral in the West had its own highly-trained choir, led by its own choirmaster and organist, who was normally a composer too. Performing standards gradually improved and the music became increasingly elaborate. In the great churches, performances at the major festivals became more like concerts than services; so much so that one pope ordered a stop to performances by exhibitionist musicians.

The mass

But elaborate church music continued to be written — particularly settings of parts of the mass. These were played in the great churches and cathedrals for special church festivals. But inevitably they had the feel of 'performances', calling for large choirs and orchestras. Today they are normally performed in concert halls by professional musicians.

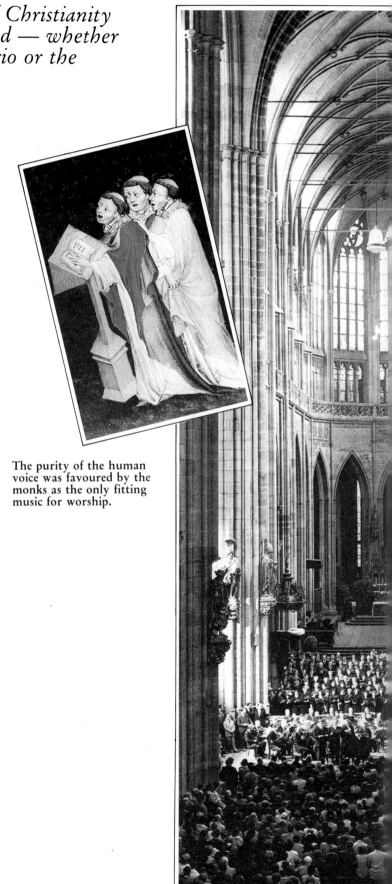

The purity of the human voice was favoured by the monks as the only fitting music for worship.

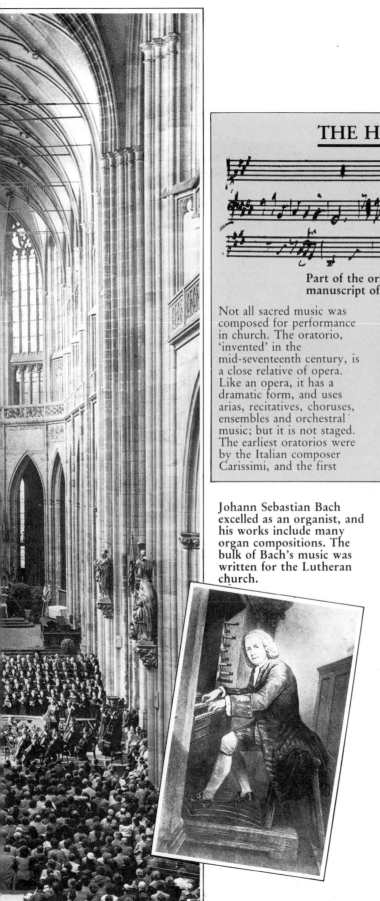

Johann Sebastian Bach excelled as an organist, and his works include many organ compositions. The bulk of Bach's music was written for the Lutheran church.

THE HALLELUJAH CHORUS

Part of the original manuscript of Handel's *Messiah*: the famous aria 'I know that my Redeemer liveth'.

Not all sacred music was composed for performance in church. The oratorio, 'invented' in the mid-seventeenth century, is a close relative of opera. Like an opera, it has a dramatic form, and uses arias, recitatives, choruses, ensembles and orchestral music; but it is not staged. The earliest oratorios were by the Italian composer Carissimi, and the first significant German examples by Schütz. J.S. Bach's *Passions* — *St John* and *St Matthew* — are similar in form, and retell the events of Holy Week.

The best-known English oratorios are by Handel: *Saul*, *Samson* and above all *Messiah*. During the writing of the celebrated 'Hallelujah Chorus' for *Messiah*, the overwhelmed composer declared: 'I did think I did see Heaven opened and the great God himself.'

Almost equally famous is Haydn's *Creation*, an oratorio in classical style, as well as Mendelssohn's *Elijah*. Twentieth-century English composers have contributed such works as *The Dream of Gerontius* (Edward Elgar), a setting of a long poem by Cardinal Newman, and *Belshazzar's Feast* (William Walton).

Some of the greatest settings of the mass are those by J.S. Bach (*Mass in B Minor*), Haydn, Mozart, Beethoven (*Missa Solemnis*), Schubert and Bruckner. Some of the profoundest settings have been of the Mass for the Dead — or Requiem; for instance, Verdi's operatic *Requiem*, Berlioz' *Grande Messe des Morts* and Benjamin Britten's *War Requiem*.

Wide appeal

Christian music is not confined to the church and concert hall. Noisy, colourful processions feature in Christian festivals throughout the world — especially in Spain and Latin America.

Similar events attracted the people of medieval Europe. In addition to music from choirboys, religious plays were performed — at first inside the church buildings, later outside in the market-place. Craftsmen's guilds would mount their own plays, and music was provided at appropriate points: for the angel choirs, the trumpet on Judgement Day and so on. Perhaps our modern equivalents are such shows as *Godspell* and *Jesus Christ Superstar*.

See too 'Hymns Ancient and Modern', page 56

ENGLAND AWAKENED

'I have only one point of view — to promote, so far as I am able, vital, practical religion; and by the grace of God, beget, preserve, and increase the life of God in the soul of men.' John Wesley

Small of stature, the 'apostle of England' John Wesley (centre) was a giant in the eighteenth-century revival movement. He was a tireless traveller: this engraving shows him returning from preaching at Castle Hill, Edinburgh, in 1790.

John Wesley affirmed his faith in this letter: 'I am not as a reed shaken by the Wind. My yea is yea, and my nay is nay. I have been firm to the Church from my youth up . . .'

The Anglican church sank into torpor in eighteenth-century England. The clergy were corrupt and indolent; 6,000 parishes were without a priest. The church did little to meet the spiritual needs of the new urban population created by the Industrial Revolution.

Man for the hour

One man did much to turn the tide: John Wesley, born into the family of a Lincolnshire priest in 1703. He was brought up piously, and continued strict religious observances in a group dubbed the 'Holy Club' while a student at Oxford. Undismayed by the mockery such a club attracted, Wesley went to America to evangelize the colonists and native Indians. But he failed in his purpose, and returned to England disillusioned.

That very year his life was revolutionized. On 24 May 1738, at a meeting in Aldersgate Street, London, during a reading from Luther's preface to Romans, he felt his heart 'strangely warmed'. Wesley experienced the 'new birth' for himself. He was set on fire to preach repentance and salvation.

Opposition

But his simple message affronted many parish ministers, who barred him from their pulpits. Nothing daunted, Wesley took to field-preaching, a practice which his able contemporary George Whitefield had successfully pioneered. John Wesley set out on horseback to preach wherever he could gather an audience. Before his death he travelled some 250,000 miles, speaking to open-air gatherings of up to 30,000 people. He crossed the Irish Sea forty-two times, and preached more than 40,000 sermons.

Wesley's meetings were frequently interrupted; the town-crier would shout, horns blow, or cows be driven into the crowd. But frequently he overcame hostile mobs:

'My heart was filled with love, my eyes with tears and my mouth with arguments. They were amazed, they were ashamed, they were melted down, they devoured my words. What a turn was this!'

As opposition grew and churches refused him entry, John Wesley took the gospel message to market squares and open spaces. Crowds flocked to hear him.

The Methodists

Wesley realized that his converts needed support in their new life. Weekly classes were organized, where they could recount trials, failures and triumphs. Here lay the foundations of the Methodist Church; for although Wesley himself never left the Church of England, the Methodists sprang from his movement.

Although some feared Methodism would be a revolutionary movement, it soon became part of established society. Wesley himself was a High Tory, and he urged loyalty and frugality on his followers. Methodism soon expanded to become one of the great denominations, notable for its stress on evangelism and on holy living.

Methodism soon spread to the New World. Wesley appointed Thomas Coke as Superintendent in North America, with the power to ordain others.

John Wesley's brother, Charles, contributed to Methodism by his vast outpouring of hymns. Until his time, Anglicans had only sung psalms; Charles wrote countless hymns to celebrate the joys and difficulties of new life in Christ.

IN GOD WE TRUST

American Protestantism expanded along with the frontier, giving it a characteristic flavour in 'the land of the free and home of the brave'.

Seven out of ten American citizens label themselves Protestant. US churches send out armies of missionaries into the world, and finance hundreds of evangelistic organizations. Protestantism has been the dominant spiritual force in American history for the last 300 years.

Freedom of religion

The US Constitution of 1776 offered the revolutionary freedom of religion to her citizens. This was despite the fact that Protestantism had reached a low ebb at that time: it had been sapped of its strength by the rationalism and tolerant apathy of Enlightenment thinkers.

    The new Republic was to have no established church. Every person was free to worship God in his own way. One result is that America can stake a good claim to having a denomination for everybody, for every outlook, for every purpose.

    From the outset these many denominations and churches faced a vast task: the christianizing of a continent, nine-tenths of it as yet uncolonized. The task was achieved with boundless energy and enterprise, by means of revivalism and missionary evangelism. Itinerant evangelists, interdenominational 'camp-meetings' and 'revivals' all contributed to the mushrooming of the Protestant denominations.

Faith on the frontier

The revival movement prospered on the American frontier, which expanded steadily throughout the nineteenth century. Methodist travelling preachers ('Circuit-riders') proclaimed the message of salvation wherever they found an audience — in barns, in taverns, in the market-place. Revivalists sought to re-kindle the spiritual devotion of the rural population at 'camp-meetings' (the first of which was held in Kentucky in about 1801). As the frontier was pushed westwards, farmer-ministers would gather fellow-believers into a new church; the revival-fire spread rapidly. Every crossroads in the American West was soon marked by its new church steeple.

A nineteenth-century US Methodist field-preacher gathers an eager audience.

Moody (left, preaching) and Sankey (right, at harmonium) enjoyed great success leading revival campaigns. Their style and organization were to have a long-term influence on mass evangelism.

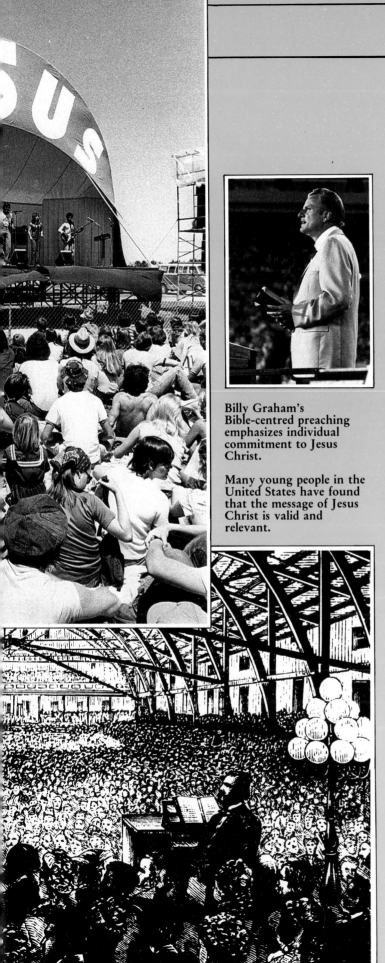

Billy Graham's Bible-centred preaching emphasizes individual commitment to Jesus Christ.

Many young people in the United States have found that the message of Jesus Christ is valid and relevant.

Save all you can

The revivalists also had to take account of the newly-developing cities of America. Charles Finney, one of the earliest American evangelists, began to adapt his revivalist methods, first to small cities, and then to New York, Boston and other metropolitan areas by 1830.

Finney's best-known successor was Dwight L. Moody (1837–99) who made his reputation as an evangelist during a successful preaching tour of Britain in 1873–75. He spent the remainder of his career conducting revival campaigns, whose success derived both from his preaching ability and from his efficient organization, and, of course, from his soloist partner Ira D. Sankey. He said: 'I look upon this world as a wrecked vessel. God has given me a lifeboat and said to me "Moody, save all you can."'

An ex-ball player, Billy Sunday, followed Moody's pattern in the early twentieth century. His raucous, flamboyant preaching was heard by a total of 100 millions; his message included a campaign against alcohol and evolution.

Billy Graham

In the 1950s appeared the most successful Christian mass-evangelist in history: Billy Graham (born in 1918). He began his urban preaching 'crusades' at a period of Protestant recovery in the USA, and mobilized all the forces of American business and communications to achieve his goal: mass-meetings, mail-shots, radio-spots, TV sponsored programmes, mass-advertising and professional public relations. Since the early 1950s, he has held countless urban crusades across the USA and in major cities throughout the non-communist world. He declared in 1952:

'I believe that America is the last bulwark of Christian civilization ... but until this nation humbles itself and prays and ... receives Christ as Savior, there is no hope for preserving the American way of life.'

HYMNS ANCIENT AND MODERN

'Sing to the Lord, all the world! Worship the Lord with joy; come before him with happy songs.'
Psalm 100

Hymn-singing — praising God in song — has been a feature of Christian worship from the very beginning. At first a 'hymn' was any song of worship; later the word was restricted to specially-written poems, as distinct from psalms and other arrangements of passages from the Bible.

At first, Christians of the Syrian, Byzantine and Armenian churches made much more of hymns than the Christians in the West. Their ancient 'Oxyrhynchus Hymn' dates back as early as about AD 300. Hilary, Bishop of Poitiers (who died about 367) is credited with writing the first hymns in the West; Ambrose of Milan followed with a number of popular and simple hymns.

Pop song tunes

Martin Luther, leader of the German Reformation, wrote many hymns himself and encouraged others to do so. He wanted to ensure that everybody could join in worship. Many of these hymns were psalms rewritten in rhyme, and set to folk-tunes or even old plainsong chants. Luther scandalized some pious Germans by setting new Christian lyrics to popular love-songs — for instance the Easter hymn, 'O sacred Head, now wounded'.

The simple Lutheran hymns deliberately contrasted with the complex music of the medieval church. The devout Lutheran composer J.S. Bach used 'chorales' from these hymns in his church cantatas, written for soloists, choir and orchestra for performance at various seasons in the church's calendar. Among at least 295 cantatas he composed, mainly while cantor at Leipzig, is the celebrated 'Jesu, Joy of Man's Desiring'.

In Britain, the earliest writers of hymn tunes were Thomas Tallis and Orlando Gibbons. Scotland followed the lead of reformers such as Calvin in keeping to settings of the psalms. In England it was in the eighteenth century that a strong tradition of hymn-writing was started, influenced by the German Moravians. Isaac Watts wrote 'When I survey the wondrous cross', John Newton 'Amazing grace', and above all the Wesley brothers wrote hundreds of hymns such as 'Love divine, all loves excelling'.

But hymn-singing was uncommon in the

Church of England until the nineteenth century. Then *Hymns Ancient and Modern*, with its many new tunes for the first time in four-part harmony, another innovation, helped introduce the idea.

The early English settlers in North America often sang their hymns to English folk-melodies. Variations on these can still be heard in gospel songs in remote areas of the South.

Expressions of faith

Most people enjoy hymn-singing; it expresses Christian hopes and beliefs simply and joyously. The Wesleys and William Booth, founder of the Salvation Army, clearly realized this. They introduced rousing hymns to express the

When I survey the wondrous cross
On which the Prince of Glory died,
My richest gain I count but loss,
And pour contempt on all my pride.

Forbid it, Lord, that I should boast
Save in the death of Christ my God;
All the vain things that charm me most,
I sacrifice them to his blood.

See from his head, his hands, his feet,
Sorrow and love flow mingled down;
Did e'er such love and sorrow meet?
Or thorns compose so rich a crown?

Were the whole realm of nature mine,
That were a present far too small;
Love so amazing, so divine
Demands my soul, my life, my all.

Isaac Watts (1674–1748)

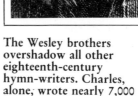

The Wesley brothers overshadow all other eighteenth-century hymn-writers. Charles, alone, wrote nearly 7,000 hymns.

Love divine, all loves excelling,
Joy of heaven, to earth come down,
Fix in us thy humble dwelling,
All thy faithful mercies crown.
Jesus, thou art all compassion,
Pure, unbounded love thou art;
Visit us with thy salvation,
Enter every longing heart.

Come, almighty to deliver,
Let us all thy life receive;
Suddenly return, and never,
Never more thy temples leave.
Thee we would be always blessing,
Serve thee as thy hosts above,
Pray, and praise thee, without ceasing,
Glory in thy perfect love.

Finish then thy new creation:
Pure and spotless may we be;
Let us see thy great salvation,
Perfectly restored in thee.
Changed from glory into glory,
Till in heaven we take our place,
Till we cast our crowns before thee,
Lost in wonder, love and praise.

Charles Wesley (1707–88)

new-found joy and assurance of their converts. In the USA too, camp-meeting evangelists and campaign revivalists such as Moody and Sankey wrote bouncy new hymns — for example, the frequently-reprinted collection of *Sacred Songs and Solos*.

Today all the major Protestant denominations have a hymn-book of their own — though many of the hymns included are shared among the different church groups. Guitar groups, rock bands and soloists have drawn on the rich tradition of the negro spiritual and black gospel music. In other parts of the world, Christians have expressed their faith in their own way and in their own music.

THE RUSSIAN CHURCH

As the Russian church developed its own traditions, it frequently crossed swords with the state — a historical fact which is also modern reality in a regime now totally hostile to Christianity.

Ivan the Terrible (−1584), the fierce despot of Russia, pushed back the boundaries of his territories, annexing Siberia and gaining control of the Volga river. He let the church profit by this expansion, and Moscow's importance as a centre of Orthodox Christianity increased. Ivan also founded new monasteries; Russian Orthodoxy had become a force to be reckoned with.

The Orthodox church resisted Western attempts to bring it under Roman influence. A Confession of Faith was drawn up in the seventeenth century to underline the uniqueness of Russian Orthodoxy.

The church had its own reformer in the great Patriarch Nikon of Moscow (−1681), who made many innovations despite the opposition of the 'Old Believers', later persecuted as schismatics.

Rule of the state

Peter the Great's efforts to drag Russia into the modern West extended even to the church. He interfered increasingly in church matters, making the church virtually another department of state. Church revenues came under state control; priests became virtual civil servants, despised by the people. But Peter also reorganized schools and monasteries, renewed parish life, and rethought religious education.

In 1721 Peter the Great abolished the traditional system of patriarchs, replacing it with a synod of bishops, controlled by a lay-person, controlled in turn by the Tsar. Thus the church became inextricably linked with the Romanov family. When the dynasty fell in 1917, the church toppled with it.

Breakaway believers

But alongside the official church were groups of Christians seeking greater holiness and separation from the all-pervading state. The Old Believers, for example, who were convinced that the end of the world was near, repudiated the hierarchy of the institutional church. When the world did not end, as prophesied, many of these radicals formed communities without priests and sacraments — but with plenty of new messiahs.

Evangelical groups similar to those in the West were also formed — known today as Baptists and the Union of Evangelical Christians. Other more mystical or puritanical sects sprang up too: the Khlysty, the Skoptsy, the Dukhobors.

Revolution

The 1917 Revolution brought the church into bondage. After 1928, each successive 'Five Year Plan' brought stricter control. Most churches were requisitioned for alternative use, and proselytizing was prohibited.

The Soviet Constitution of 1929 guaranteed 'the freedom to hold religious services and the freedom of anti-religious propaganda'. This is interpreted literally: any citizen may worship inside a building registered for worship; but many Christians continue to spread their faith regardless.

Most Russian Christians are still Orthodox. Although many of their church buildings have been closed, they continue to worship with traditional fervour. And the groups of evangelical Christians are as active and live today as ever, despite all the efforts of the state, by persecution, repression and propaganda, to stamp them out.

TO THE JUNGLES — AND CITIES

After nineteen centuries of only sporadic attempts to 'go out into all the world' to convert people to Christ, the modern missionary movement has mushroomed, taking the gospel all over the world by a great army of people, by educational and medical work, by literature, radio and television . . .

On 31 May 1792, a village cobbler in Northamptonshire, England, preached on the theme: 'Expect great things from God, and attempt great things for God'. It was a time of exploration and national expansion. This English Baptist, William Carey, was one of the pioneers of the modern missionary movement.

Carey continued writing and preaching, forming missionary societies, and eventually, with Joshua Marshman and William Ward, went out to India as a missionary himself. He landed at Calcutta in 1793, and set out to learn the languages, translate the Bible, make converts and liberalize Indian laws and customs. An indefatigable worker, he never returned to Britain.

Anglicans soon followed the Baptist example, despite discouragement from the British East India Company, which did not want trade hampered by religious busy-bodies. Henry Martyn, a brilliant scholar, said he would burn himself out for Christ; he died at thirty-one, after heroic labours in India and Persia.

Carey virtually invented the missionary society — a voluntary body for sending missionaries abroad. His own Baptist Missionary Society was the first in the field, rapidly followed by the London Missionary Society in 1795, the Scottish Missionary Society (1796) and the Church Missionary Society — and many others, both Protestant and Catholic.

The story of early missionary outreach is one of heroism, adventure, love for all peoples, and faith in reaching them for Christ.

STORMING URBAN STRONGHOLDS

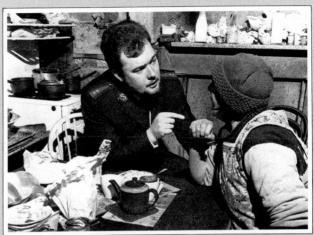

Members of the Salvation Army bring help to the destitute and a gospel of hope for the poor.

Britain was the first industrial nation. Industrialization brought burgeoning cities, mushrooming towns, and vast new urban populations. The cities sucked in workers from the rural areas, and housed them in miserable close-packed terraces.

Here was an immense new problem for the church. There were attempts to create new parish churches, but little was done to cater for the special needs of those who felt rootless in their new surroundings. Often the Methodists were best equipped to reach the urban working classes, with their simple church buildings, lay preachers and straightforward teachings.

But the mass of the working classes was neglected by the churches. One response to the problem was to send 'missionaries' into the urban jungle. The London City Mission was established early in the nineteenth century to 'win souls' who could be integrated into their neighbourhood parish church. Such missions were duplicated in most of the great cities.

More colourful, effective and famous was William Booth's Salvation Army. Booth brought imagination, organizational wizardry, charismatic leadership and undying zeal to the task. He was motivated by a horror of sin and a hatred of squalor. He had a basic message of repentance and salvation, and a rumbustious organization which appealed by its militaristic methods and joyous extroversion.

Booth was never afraid of being popular. He used working-class leaders and evangelists. He used brass bands and music-hall tunes. He used colourful personalities such as the 'Sacred Barmaid' and a redeemed escapologist. He was so successful, not least in saving people from drunkenness, that enraged publicans and brewers often organized violent opposition to his street-meetings.

The Army was started in 1865. Booth's organizing genius ran to emigration schemes, soup-kitchens, hostels for the unemployed, social-work brigades and a whole battery of first-aid measures. The Salvation Army is still honoured worldwide for its readiness to respond to human problems — homelessness, disasters, accidents and addictions.

The methods of the Salvation Army were widely copied — by the Anglicans' Church Army, and by many militaristic church youth organizations.

OUTREACH AND UNITY

It is urgent that the gospel be taken to all nations. It is also urgent that Western church patterns, and particularly Western church divisions, are not taken at the same time. In the West, how can the scars of history be healed 'so that the church may be one'?

Bishop Azariah of India voiced the feelings of many twentieth-century Christians when he said in 1937:

'We want you to take us seriously when we say that the problem of union is one of life and death with us.'

The scandal of division was a growing obstacle to belief, and a deepening source of shame.

But moves towards unity were already proceeding. In the late nineteenth century, the American John Mott enthused the interdenominational Student Christian Movement with his message of world mission. The YMCA gave birth to the World Student Christian Federation in 1895, which, with the Student Volunteer Movement, provided some of the great prophets of unity. The SVM's vision was summed up in the motto, 'The Evangelization of the World in this Generation'. With the emphasis on world mission, the problems of disunity were in focus.

New churches worldwide

Gradually the worst features of missionary colonialism were repaired: national churches developed as independence was gained.

The churches were spurred by World War II to reconvene in 1948 to form the World Council of Churches in Amsterdam. The headquarters were later moved to Geneva, and a series of assemblies in various continents followed; Amsterdam, Evanston, New Delhi, Uppsala and Nairobi.

But as yet this was no true World Council: Roman Catholics and Russian Orthodox were notable absentees. However, Pope John XXIII changed the face of things with his call for 'that unity for which Jesus Christ prayed', and his summoning of the Vatican II Council (1962–65) to renew the Roman Catholic church. A new openness to ecumenical affairs had come to the Catholic church.

Grass-roots unity

But worldwide ecumenism was also reflected in a grass-roots trend towards unity. As early as 1927, five denominations in China gathered in one Church of Christ. Later, and more famously, the Anglicans, Methodists, Presbyterians, Congregationalists and Reformed joined to form the Church of South India, a model for many others. The United Church of Canada appeared as a merger of several denominations in 1925, and many smaller denominations combined with one another in the USA.

And at a local level Christians of differing traditions take it for granted that they will work and pray and evangelize together. Home Bible study groups, young people's meetings, student groups in colleges and universities, relief work and missions, demonstrate that for many their shared life in Christ is more important to them than their denominational tradition.

Following two disastrous cyclones in southern India, funds from the relief agency TEAR Fund helped local Christians from many churches to build houses and establish fishing and woodwork projects. Demonstrating the love of God by relieving human suffering and improving the quality of life unites Christians in a common purpose which transcends denominational barriers.

OPEN DOORS

Worshippers leave a recently re-opened Christian chapel in Canton in the People's Republic of China.

SURVIVAL IN COMMUNIST CHINA

In 1807 Robert Morrison led the first Protestant assault on China. Although he made few converts, he produced a translation of the Bible in Chinese. Inter-church Protestant missions and Roman Catholic orders soon followed, although Chinese domestic policy posed peculiar problems.

James Hudson Taylor's China Inland Mission was one of the pioneers. Depending for all money on God alone, he refused to advertise for support; he also experimented with 'going native' in costume. The Boxer Rebellion in 1900 was a violent nationalist reaction against missionary colonialism; it was second only to the 1947 Maoist Revolution in its damage to Western Christian activities.

Now, however, Chinese groups of Christians are re-surfacing. The church has survived thirty years of opposition, persecution and militant propaganda.